The Ultimate Hamilton Beach Dual Breakfast Sandwich Maker Cookbook

365 Days of Healthy Tasty Hamburger Recipes for Busy Beginners Cooking – Family-Friendly Omelets, Muffins, and More!

Asoldy Nontegue

Table of Contents

INTRODUCTION

What is Hamilton Beach Breakfast Sandwich Maker?

The Hamilton Beach Breakfast Sandwich Maker is a kitchen appliance designed to streamline the process of preparing homemade breakfast sandwiches. It is a compact, easy-to-use device that allows users to create a hot and customized breakfast sandwich in under 5 minutes. The appliance consists of several key components that work together seamlessly to facilitate the sandwich-making process.

Design and Components:

- The Breakfast Sandwich Maker typically consists of four main parts:

  Bottom Layer (Base): This is where the base of the sandwich is assembled. Users can place a variety of ingredients such as bread, English muffins, or bagels in this section.

  Egg Cooking Plate: Positioned above the bottom layer, this is where the egg is cooked. Users crack an egg onto the cooking plate, and the heat from the appliance cooks it to the desired level of doneness.

  Top Layer (Lid): The top layer contains a cooking plate that presses down on the assembled ingredients. It also has a handle to facilitate easy opening and closing of the appliance.

  Slide-Out Tray: After the sandwich is assembled and cooked, this tray

Quick and Easy
Just four simple steps, ready in five minutes

can be slid out, allowing the user to easily access and remove the finished breakfast sandwich.

Operation:

- Using the Hamilton Beach Breakfast Sandwich Maker is a straightforward process:

  Assemble Ingredients: Place the chosen bread or base in the bottom layer, add desired ingredients such as cheese, ham, or vegetables, and crack an egg onto the cooking plate.

Close Lid: Once the ingredients are in place, close the lid to start the cooking process. The heat from the appliance cooks the egg and warms the other ingredients simultaneously.

Slide Out Tray: After a few minutes, the user can slide out the tray, revealing a fully assembled and cooked breakfast sandwich.

Enjoy: Open the lid, and the hot and ready-to-eat breakfast sandwich is ready to be enjoyed.

The Breakfast Sandwich Maker often comes with a recipe book that provides users with a variety of options for creating different types of

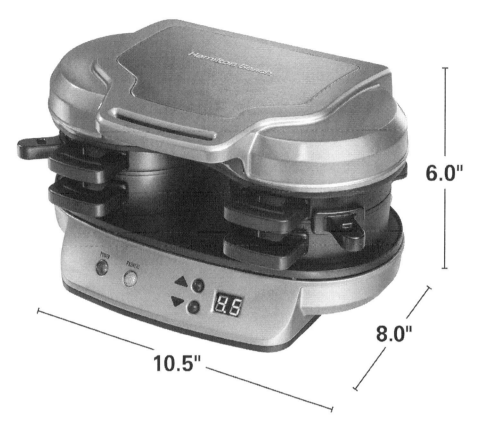

Hamilton Beach

6.0"

8.0"

10.5"

Dual Breakfast Sandwich Maker

breakfast sandwiches. The recipes range from classic combinations like egg, ham, and cheese to more unique and gourmet choices, such as a cheddar, apple, bacon, and egg croissant sandwich. This adds an element of versatility to the appliance, allowing users to explore various flavor profiles and tailor their breakfast sandwiches to their preferences.

One of the key features of the Hamilton Beach Breakfast Sandwich Maker is its versatility. Users can experiment with different ingredients, making it easy to cater to individual tastes and dietary preferences. The appliance's compact design also makes it a convenient addition to any kitchen, particularly for those with busy lifestyles who still want a homemade and hot breakfast.

In summary, the Hamilton Beach Breakfast Sandwich Maker is a user-friendly kitchen appliance that simplifies the process of preparing customized and hot breakfast sandwiches. With its intuitive design, efficient cooking process, and included recipe book, it offers a convenient solution for individuals and families looking to enjoy a quick and tasty breakfast at home.

Benefits of Using Hamilton Beach Breakfast Sandwich Maker

The Hamilton Beach Breakfast Sandwich Maker offers a range of benefits that contribute to its popularity among consumers seeking a quick and convenient breakfast solution. Here are several key advantages:

- Time Efficiency:

  One of the primary benefits of the Breakfast Sandwich Maker is its ability to produce a hot and customized breakfast sandwich in under 5 minutes. The appliance's efficient heating elements and design allow users to simultaneously cook the egg and warm the other ingredients, reducing the overall cooking time compared to traditional stovetop methods. This time efficiency is particularly valuable for individuals with busy mornings who still want to enjoy a homemade breakfast.

- Ease of Use:

The Breakfast Sandwich Maker is designed with simplicity in mind. Its four-step process—assemble ingredients, close lid, slide out tray, and enjoy—makes it accessible even for those with limited cooking skills. The appliance eliminates the need for multiple pans and utensils, streamlining the cooking process and minimizing cleanup time. The straightforward operation contributes to the appliance's user-friendly nature.

- Customization and Versatility:

The appliance's modular design allows for a high degree of customization. Users can choose their preferred bread or base, add a variety of ingredients such as meats, cheeses, and vegetables, and adjust the egg's cooking time to achieve the desired level of doneness. The inclusion of a recipe book further enhances versatility, providing inspiration for a wide range of breakfast sandwich combinations. This customization aspect caters to individual tastes and dietary preferences, making the Breakfast Sandwich Maker a versatile addition to any kitchen.

- Compact Design:

The compact and space-saving design of the Breakfast Sandwich Maker is advantageous for individuals with limited kitchen space. Its small footprint makes it suitable for apartments, dorm rooms, or kitchens with minimal counter space. The appliance's portability also makes it a convenient option for those who may want to bring it to work or other locations, ensuring a hot and satisfying breakfast is always within reach.

- Healthy Options:

For individuals conscious of their dietary choices, the Breakfast Sandwich Maker allows for the inclusion of fresh and wholesome ingredients. Users have the flexibility to incorporate whole-grain bread, lean proteins, and a variety of vegetables, promoting healthier breakfast choices. The appliance's quick cooking time also ensures that nutrients in the ingredients are retained, contributing to a nutritious start to the day.

- Cost-Effective:

The Hamilton Beach Breakfast Sandwich Maker offers a cost-effective solution for those who prefer homemade breakfasts over purchasing pre-made options or dining out. By using readily available and affordable ingredients, users can create delicious breakfast sandwiches at a fraction of the cost of buying prepared meals. This cost-effectiveness, combined with the appliance's time-saving benefits, makes it an attractive option for budget-conscious individuals and families.

- Family-Friendly:

  The Breakfast Sandwich Maker is well-suited for families with diverse tastes. Each family member can customize their sandwich according to personal preferences, accommodating varying dietary restrictions and preferences. The simplicity of the appliance's operation also makes it suitable for older children and teenagers who may want to prepare their own breakfasts.

In conclusion, the Hamilton Beach Breakfast Sandwich Maker offers a range of benefits, including time efficiency, ease of use, customization, compact design, healthy options, cost-effectiveness, and family-friendliness. These advantages make it a popular and practical choice for individuals and families seeking a quick, convenient, and customizable breakfast solution.

The Step-by-Step Procedure of Using the Hamilton Beach Breakfast Sandwich Maker

Using the Hamilton Beach Breakfast Sandwich Maker is a straightforward process, and with a few simple steps, you can enjoy a delicious homemade breakfast sandwich in under 5 minutes. Here's a detailed step-by-step procedure:

- Step 1: Gather Ingredients

  Before you begin, gather all the ingredients you want to include in your breakfast sandwich. This can include bread, eggs, cheese, meat, vegetables, and any other toppings of your choice.

- Step 2: Preheat the Sandwich Maker

  Plug in the Hamilton Beach Breakfast Sandwich Maker and allow it to preheat. Most models have an indicator light that will let you know when it's ready for use. Preheating ensures that your sandwich cooks evenly and efficiently.

- Step 3: Prepare the Bottom Layer

  Open the lid of the sandwich maker and place the bottom half of your chosen bread on the bottom plate. This serves as the base of your sandwich. You can use English muffins, bagels, croissants, or any bread of your preference.

- Step 4: Add Ingredients

  Layer your ingredients on top of the bottom bread slice. Start with your choice of protein, such as ham, bacon, or sausage. Add cheese and any other desired toppings, like vegetables or avocado. Be creative and experiment with different combinations.

- Step 5: Crack an Egg

  Carefully crack an egg onto the cooking plate. If you prefer a scrambled egg, you can beat it first before pouring it onto the plate. Close the lid gently to let the egg cook.

- Step 6: Cook the Egg

  Allow the egg to cook for a few minutes until it reaches your desired level of doneness. The cooking time may vary depending on the model and the specific settings of your sandwich maker.

- Step 7: Add the Top Layer

  Once the egg is cooked, slide out the cooking plate to reveal the assembled sandwich. Place the top half of your bread on top of the egg to complete the sandwich.

- Step 8: Remove and Enjoy

  Carefully open the lid and use a spatula to lift the hot breakfast sandwich from the machine. Be cautious, as the sandwich maker and the contents will be hot. Your delicious homemade breakfast sandwich is now ready to be enjoyed.

- Step 9: Clean the Sandwich Maker

  After enjoying your meal, unplug the sandwich maker and allow it to cool. The non-stick surfaces of the cooking plates make for easy cleaning. Wipe them down with a damp cloth or sponge, and if they are removable, wash them in warm, soapy water.

Tips and Tricks for Cooking Success

While using the Hamilton Beach Breakfast Sandwich Maker is relatively simple, there are some tips and tricks to enhance your cooking experience and ensure the best results:

- Tip 1: Experiment with Ingredients

  Don't be afraid to get creative with your breakfast sandwich fillings. Try different combinations of meats, cheeses, and vegetables to discover your favorite flavor profile. The recipe book included with the sandwich maker can provide inspiration for unique and tasty combinations.

- Tip 2: Preheat for Optimal Results

  Allow the sandwich maker to preheat fully before adding your ingredients. This ensures that your sandwich cooks evenly and quickly. The indicator light will signal when the machine is ready, so be patient and let it reach the desired temperature.

- Tip 3: Use Cooking Spray

  To prevent your sandwich from sticking to the cooking plates, consider lightly spraying them with cooking spray before assembling your ingredients. This step can make it easier to remove the finished sandwich without any sticking.

- Tip 4: Customize Cooking Time

  Adjust the cooking time based on your preferences for egg doneness. If you like a runny yolk, you may cook the egg for a shorter duration. For a fully cooked egg, leave it in a bit longer. Experiment to find the perfect balance for your taste.

- Tip 5: Layer Ingredients Thoughtfully

  Layering your ingredients strategically can impact the overall texture and taste of your sandwich.

Placing cheese next to the bread can prevent it from becoming too soggy, while placing it on top of the egg allows it to melt and blend with the other flavors.

- Tip 6: Keep It Compact

  Avoid overloading the sandwich maker with ingredients. A moderate amount of fillings ensures that the sandwich cooks evenly and that the lid closes properly. Overfilling may result in an unevenly cooked or messy sandwich.

- Tip 7: Prepare Ingredients in Advance

  To streamline the breakfast-making process, consider preparing some ingredients in advance. Pre-cook meats, chop vegetables, or pre-crack eggs to save time in the morning rush.

- Tip 8: Clean Regularly

  Regular cleaning is essential for maintaining the performance and longevity of your sandwich maker. Follow the manufacturer's instructions for cleaning, and be sure to remove any leftover crumbs or residue after each use.

- Tip 9: Get Creative with Toppings

  Enhance the flavor of your breakfast sandwich by adding toppings after cooking. Fresh herbs, hot sauce, or a drizzle of your favorite condiment can elevate the taste and add a personal touch.

- Tip 10: Double-check Safety Features

  Familiarize yourself with the safety features of your specific Hamilton Beach Breakfast Sandwich Maker. Ensure that it has cooled down before cleaning, and be cautious when handling hot surfaces. Following the safety guidelines provided by the manufacturer is crucial for a safe cooking experience.

In conclusion, the Hamilton Beach Breakfast Sandwich Maker offers a convenient and quick way to enjoy a customized breakfast sandwich. By following the step-by-step procedure and incorporating these tips and tricks into your cooking routine, you can create delicious and personalized breakfast sandwiches with ease. Experiment with different ingredients, explore new flavor combinations, and make the most of this versatile kitchen appliance.

Important Safety Reminders & Troubleshooting Guide

- Read the User Manual:

  Before using the Hamilton Beach Breakfast Sandwich Maker, it is crucial

to thoroughly read the user manual provided by the manufacturer. The manual contains essential information about the appliance's features, assembly, and operating instructions. Ignoring the manual may result in improper use and potential safety hazards.

- Proper Assembly:

Ensure that the Breakfast Sandwich Maker is correctly assembled before use. Check that all parts are securely connected and in their designated positions. Misassembly can lead to malfunctions and safety risks. Pay special attention to the cooking plate, lid, and base alignment to prevent any accidents during operation.

- Power Source:

Verify that the appliance is connected to a suitable power source that meets the specified voltage requirements. Avoid using extension cords or power outlets with a different voltage to prevent electrical malfunctions or damage to the Breakfast Sandwich Maker. Always plug the appliance directly into a compatible outlet.

- Position on a Stable Surface:

Place the Breakfast Sandwich Maker on a stable, flat surface during use. Ensure that it is not positioned near the edge of a countertop or any other unstable surface. This prevents accidental tipping or falling, reducing the risk of injuries or damage to the appliance.

- Handle with Caution:

The appliance can become hot during operation. Use caution when handling the Breakfast Sandwich Maker, especially when opening the lid or removing the cooked sandwich. Always use oven mitts or other protective tools to avoid burns or injuries.

- Cleaning and Maintenance:

Before cleaning the appliance, unplug it and let it cool down. Clean the non-stick cooking surfaces with a soft, damp cloth. Avoid using abrasive materials or harsh chemicals that may damage the non-stick coating. Regular maintenance contributes to the longevity of the Breakfast Sandwich Maker and ensures safe, hygienic food preparation.

- Ventilation:

The Breakfast Sandwich Maker is equipped with ventilation openings to prevent overheating. Ensure that these openings are not blocked during use. Adequate ventilation is crucial for the appliance's proper functioning and prevents the risk of overheating or malfunction.

- Children and Pets:

Keep the appliance out of reach of children and pets, especially during operation. The surfaces can become hot, posing a burn risk. Additionally, curious children may accidentally touch or tamper with the appliance, leading to injuries or damage.

Troubleshooting Guide for the Hamilton Beach Breakfast Sandwich Maker:

- Appliance Not Powering On:

Check the power source and ensure that the Breakfast Sandwich Maker is properly plugged in.

Verify that the outlet is functional by testing with another appliance.

If the issue persists, contact the manufacturer's customer support for further assistance.

- Uneven Cooking:

Ensure that the ingredients are distributed evenly on the cooking plate.

Check for any misalignment of the cooking plate, lid, or base that may affect even cooking.

Adjust the ingredients to create a uniform sandwich thickness.

- Sticking Issues:

Apply a small amount of cooking oil or non-stick spray to the cooking surfaces before use.

Allow the appliance to preheat adequately before placing ingredients to prevent sticking.

- Lid Difficult to Close:

Check for any obstruction or misalignment of the cooking plate that may impede the closing of the lid.

Ensure that the ingredients are within the designated boundaries to prevent interference with the lid.

- Cleaning Challenges:

Allow the appliance to cool before cleaning.

Use a soft, damp cloth for cleaning, and avoid abrasive materials or harsh chemicals.

If residue is stubborn, gently scrape it off with a non-abrasive tool.

- Unusual Smells or Smoke:

Check for any food debris or grease buildup on the heating elements.

Ensure proper ventilation and that the appliance is not placed near flammable materials.

If the issue persists, discontinue use and contact customer support.

- Inconsistent Heating:

Verify that the power source meets the appliance's requirements.

Check for any visible damage to the heating elements.

If inconsistencies persist, contact customer support for further guidance.

- Lid Won't Open:

Allow the appliance to cool down before attempting to open the lid.

Check for any obstruction or misalignment that may be preventing the lid from opening.

If the issue persists, contact customer support for assistance.

In conclusion, prioritizing safety and following the troubleshooting guide are essential for the optimal and safe use of the Hamilton Beach Breakfast Sandwich Maker. Regular maintenance, proper assembly, and adherence to safety precautions contribute to a reliable and enjoyable cooking experience with this appliance.

Chapter 1: Normal Breakfast Sandwiches and Omelets

Avocado and Bacon Omelet

Prep Time: 7 Minutes   Cook Time: 4-5 Minutes   Serves: 1

Ingredients:

- 2 large eggs
- 2 slices cooked bacon, crumbled
- 1/4 avocado, sliced
- 2 tablespoons diced tomatoes
- 2 tablespoons shredded cheddar cheese
- Salt and pepper to taste

Directions:

1. Preheat the Breakfast Sandwich Maker until the green PREHEAT light comes on.
2. Lightly scramble both eggs and pour onto the bottom ring of the maker.
3. Add crumbled bacon, sliced avocado, diced tomatoes, and shredded cheddar cheese.
4. Lower the cooking plate and top ring.
5. Close the cover and cook for 4 to 5 minutes.
6. Slide out the cooking plate and lift cover and rings; transfer the omelet to a plate using a spatula.
7. Season with salt and pepper to taste.
8. Serve hot and enjoy.

Nutritional Value (Amount per Serving):

Calories: 455; Fat: 38; Carb: 15.06; Protein: 16.11

Spinach and Sun-Dried Tomato Breakfast Sandwich

Prep Time: 8 Minutes   Cook Time: 4-5 Minutes   Serves: 1

Ingredients:

- 2 English muffins, split
- 2 large eggs
- 1/4 cup fresh baby spinach, chopped
- 2 tablespoons sun-dried tomatoes, diced
- 2 tablespoons cream cheese
- Salt and pepper to taste

Directions:

1. Preheat the Breakfast Sandwich Maker until the green PREHEAT light comes on.
2. Lift the cover, top ring, and cooking plate.
3. Place the bottom half of the English muffins on the bottom ring.
4. Lower the cooking plate and top ring.
5. Crack one egg onto the cooking plate.
6. Season eggs with salt and pepper.

7. Add chopped baby spinach, diced sun-dried tomatoes, and cream cheese.
8. Cover with the remaining English muffin half.
9. Close the cover and cook for 4 to 5 minutes.
10. Slide out the cooking plate and carefully remove the sandwich with a spatula.
11. Serve hot and enjoy.

Nutritional Value (Amount per Serving):

Calories: 499; Fat: 20.4; Carb: 63.03; Protein: 20.72

Ham and Swiss Omelet Croissant

Prep Time: 8 Minutes   Cook Time: 4-5 Minutes   Serves: 1

Ingredients:

- 1 croissant, split
- 2 large eggs
- 1/4 cup diced ham
- 2 tablespoons shredded Swiss cheese
- 1 tablespoon chopped green onions
- Salt and pepper to taste

Directions:

1. Preheat the Breakfast Sandwich Maker until the green PREHEAT light comes on.
2. Place one croissant half on the bottom ring of the maker.
3. Lower the cooking plate and top ring.
4. Lightly scramble both eggs and pour onto the cooking plate.
5. Add diced ham, shredded Swiss cheese, and chopped green onions.
6. Add other half of the croissant.
7. Close the cover and cook for 4 to 5 minutes.
8. Slide out the cooking plate and carefully fold the omelet in half.
9. Lift cover and rings; transfer the omelet to a plate using a spatula.
10. Season with salt and pepper to taste.
11. Serve hot and enjoy.

Nutritional Value (Amount per Serving):

Calories: 1182; Fat: 79.9; Carb: 37.73; Protein: 77.97

Caprese Breakfast Burrito

Prep Time: 7 Minutes   Cook Time: 4-5 Minutes   Serves: 1

Ingredients:

- 1 large flour tortilla
- 2 large eggs, beaten
- 1/4 cup diced tomatoes
- 2 tablespoons fresh mozzarella cheese, diced
- Fresh basil leaves

- Balsamic glaze for drizzling
- Salt and pepper to taste

Directions:

1. Preheat the Breakfast Sandwich Maker until the green PREHEAT light comes on.
2. Place the tortilla on the bottom ring of the maker.
3. Pour beaten eggs onto the tortilla.
4. Add diced tomatoes, diced fresh mozzarella cheese, and fresh basil leaves.
5. Lower the cooking plate and top ring.
6. Close the cover and cook for 4 to 5 minutes.
7. Slide out the cooking plate and carefully roll the burrito.
8. Lift cover and rings; transfer the burrito to a plate using a spatula.
9. Drizzle with balsamic glaze.
10. Serve warm and enjoy.

Nutritional Value (Amount per Serving):

Calories: 307; Fat: 12.16; Carb: 35.93; Protein: 14.77

Smoked Salmon and Cream Cheese Bagel Sandwich

Prep Time: 6 Minutes   Cook Time: 4-5 Minutes   Serves: 1

Ingredients:

- 1 everything bagel, split and toasted
- 2 large eggs
- 2 ounces smoked salmon
- 2 tablespoons cream cheese
- Capers and fresh dill for garnish
- Salt and pepper to taste

Directions:

1. Preheat the Breakfast Sandwich Maker until the green PREHEAT light comes on.
2. Place the toasted everything bagel half on the bottom ring of the maker.
3. Lower the cooking plate and top ring.
4. Crack one egg onto cooking plate.
5. Season eggs with salt and pepper.
6. Add smoked salmon and cream cheese on top of each egg.
7. Add the other half of bagel on top of everything.
8. Close the cover and cook for 4 to 5 minutes.
9. Slide out the cooking plate and carefully remove the sandwich with a spatula.
10. Garnish with capers and fresh dill.
11. Serve hot and enjoy.

Nutritional Value (Amount per Serving):

Calories: 589; Fat: 23.48; Carb: 63.21; Protein: 31.22

Italian Breakfast Panini

Prep Time: 8 Minutes   Cook Time: 4-5 Minutes   Serves: 1

Ingredients:

- 2 slices Italian bread
- 2 large eggs, beaten
- 2 slices prosciutto
- 2 tablespoons diced tomatoes
- 2 tablespoons shredded mozzarella cheese
- Fresh basil leaves
- Olive oil for brushing

Directions:

1. Preheat the Breakfast Sandwich Maker until the green PREHEAT light comes on.
2. Brush one side of each bread slice with olive oil.
3. Place one bread slice, olive oil side down, on the bottom ring of the maker.
4. Lower the cooking plate and top ring.
5. Pour beaten eggs onto cooking plate.
6. Add prosciutto, diced tomatoes, shredded mozzarella cheese, and fresh basil leaves.
7. Top with the second bread slice, olive oil side up.
8. Close the cover and cook for 4 to 5 minutes.
9. Slide out the cooking plate and carefully remove the panini with a spatula.
10. Serve hot and enjoy.

Nutritional Value (Amount per Serving):

Calories: 1044; Fat: 31.72; Carb: 39.44; Protein: 151.91

Mediterranean Veggie Breakfast Wrap

Prep Time: 7 Minutes   Cook Time: 4-5 Minutes   Serves: 1

Ingredients:

- 1 tortilla
- 2 large eggs, beaten
- 1/4 cup diced tomatoes
- 1/4 cup diced cucumbers
- 2 tablespoons crumbled feta cheese
- 1 tablespoon chopped Kalamata olives
- Fresh oregano for garnish
- Salt and pepper to taste

Directions:

1. Preheat the Breakfast Sandwich Maker until the green PREHEAT light comes on.
2. Place the tortilla on the bottom ring of the maker.
3. Lower the cooking plate and top ring.
4. Pour beaten eggs onto the cooking plate.
5. Add diced tomatoes, diced cucumbers, crumbled feta cheese, and chopped Kalamata olives.
6. Close the cover and cook for 4 to 5 minutes.
7. Slide out the cooking plate and carefully roll the wrap.
8. Lift cover and rings; transfer the wrap to a plate using a spatula.
9. Garnish with fresh oregano.
10. Serve warm and enjoy.

Nutritional Value (Amount per Serving):

Calories: 1082; Fat:76.82 ; Carb: 45.8; Protein: 53.4

Ranchero Breakfast Burrito

Prep Time: 8 Minutes   Cook Time: 4-5 Minutes   Serves: 1

Ingredients:

- 1 flour tortilla
- 2 large eggs, beaten
- 1/4 cup black beans, drained and rinsed
- 2 tablespoons diced tomatoes
- 2 tablespoons diced onions
- 2 tablespoons shredded pepper jack cheese
- Salsa and cilantro for topping

Directions:

1. Preheat the Breakfast Sandwich Maker until the green PREHEAT light comes on.
2. Place the tortilla on the bottom ring of the maker.
3. Lower the cooking plate and top ring.
4. Pour beaten eggs onto cooking plate.
5. Add black beans, diced tomatoes, diced onions, and shredded pepper jack cheese.
6. Close the cover and cook for 4 to 5 minutes.
7. Slide out the cooking plate and carefully roll the burrito.
8. Lift cover and rings; transfer the burrito to a plate using a spatula.
9. Top with salsa and cilantro.
10. Serve warm and enjoy.

Nutritional Value (Amount per Serving):

Calories: 1195; Fat: 81.98; Carb: 45.03; Protein: 69.73

Hawaiian Breakfast Sandwich

Prep Time: 8 Minutes   Cook Time: 4-5 Minutes   Serves: 1

Ingredients:

- 2 slices Hawaiian sweet bread
- 2 large eggs
- 2 slices Canadian bacon
- 2 slices pineapple
- 2 tablespoons shredded Swiss cheese
- Salt and pepper to taste

Directions:

1. Preheat the Breakfast Sandwich Maker until the green PREHEAT light comes on.
2. Lift the cover, top ring, and cooking plate.
3. Place one slice of Hawaiian sweet bread on the bottom ring.
4. Lower the cooking plate and top ring.
5. Crack one egg onto the cooking plate.
6. Add a slice of Canadian bacon, a slice of pineapple, and shredded Swiss cheese.
7. Top with the second slice of Hawaiian sweet bread.
8. Close the cover and cook for 4 to 5 minutes.
9. Slide out the cooking plate and carefully remove the sandwich with a spatula.
10. Season with salt and pepper to taste.
11. Serve hot and enjoy.

Nutritional Value (Amount per Serving):

Calories: 1092; Fat: 71.1; Carb: 37.59; Protein: 77.8

Mediterranean Breakfast Pita Pocket

Prep Time: 7 Minutes   Cook Time: 4-5 Minutes   Serves: 1

Ingredients:

- 1 whole wheat pita, halved
- 2 large eggs, beaten
- 1/4 cup diced cucumbers
- 1/4 cup diced tomatoes
- 2 tablespoons crumbled feta cheese

- 1 tablespoon chopped Kalamata olives
- Fresh parsley for garnish
- Salt and pepper to taste

Directions:

1. Preheat the Breakfast Sandwich Maker until the green PREHEAT light comes on.
2. Place the halved whole wheat pita on the bottom ring of the maker.
3. Lower the cooking plate and top ring.
4. Pour beaten eggs onto the cooking plate.
5. Add diced cucumbers, diced tomatoes, crumbled feta cheese, and chopped Kalamata olives.
6. Close the cover and cook for 4 to 5 minutes.
7. Slide out the cooking plate and carefully lift the pita halves with a spatula.
8. Season with salt and pepper to taste.
9. Garnish with fresh parsley.
10. Serve warm and enjoy.

Nutritional Value (Amount per Serving):

Calories: 1016; Fat: 74.76; Carb: 36.22; Protein: 52.45

Denver Omelet Breakfast Wrap

Prep Time: 8 Minutes   Cook Time: 4-5 Minutes   Serves: 1

Ingredients:

- 1 tortilla
- 2 large eggs, beaten
- 1/4 cup diced ham
- 2 tablespoons diced bell peppers (assorted colors)
- 2 tablespoons diced onions
- 2 tablespoons shredded cheddar cheese

Directions:

1. Preheat the Breakfast Sandwich Maker until the green PREHEAT light comes on.
2. Place the tortilla on the bottom ring of the maker.
3. Lower the cooking plate and top ring.
4. Pour beaten eggs onto the cooking plate.
5. Add diced ham, diced bell peppers, diced onions, and shredded cheddar cheese.
6. Close the cover and cook for 4 to 5 minutes.
7. Slide out the cooking plate and carefully roll the wrap.
8. Lift cover and rings; transfer the wrap to a plate using a spatula.

9. Serve warm and enjoy.

Nutritional Value (Amount per Serving):

Calories: 374; Fat: 15.17; Carb: 37.73; Protein: 22.63

Turkey and Cranberry Breakfast Croissant

Prep Time: 8 Minutes   Cook Time: 4-5 Minutes   Serves: 1

Ingredients:

- 1 croissant, split
- 2 large eggs
- 2 slices turkey or turkey sausage
- 2 tablespoons cranberry sauce
- 2 tablespoons shredded Gouda cheese
- Salt and pepper to taste

Directions:

1. Preheat the Breakfast Sandwich Maker until the green PREHEAT light comes on.
2. Place the croissant half on the bottom ring of the maker.
3. Lower the cooking plate and top ring.
4. Lightly scramble both eggs and pour onto the cooking plate.
5. Add slices of turkey, cranberry sauce, and shredded Gouda cheese.
6. Add the other croissant half on top of everything.
7. Close the cover and cook for 4 to 5 minutes.
8. Slide out the cooking plate and carefully fold the eggs in the croissant.
9. Lift cover and rings; transfer the croissant to a plate using a spatula.
10. Season with salt and pepper to taste.
11. Serve hot and enjoy.

Nutritional Value (Amount per Serving):

Calories: 693; Fat: 36.45; Carb: 54.48; Protein: 37.87

Chapter 2: Red Meat Sandwiches and Burgers

Bacon and Blue Cheese Bison Burger

Prep Time: 12 Minutes   Cook Time: 7-8 Minutes   Serves: 1

Ingredients:

- 1/4 pound ground bison
- 2 slices bacon, cooked
- 2 tablespoons blue cheese crumbles
- Pinch of salt
- Pinch of black pepper
- 1 hamburger bun, split

Directions:

1. Preheat Breakfast Sandwich Maker until the green PREHEAT light comes on.
2. In a bowl, mix ground bison with salt and pepper. Shape into a patty.
3. Place the patty on the bottom ring of the Breakfast Sandwich Maker.
4. Top the patty with cooked bacon and blue cheese crumbles.
5. Close the cover and cook for 7 to 8 minutes until the bison is cooked through.
6. Toast the hamburger bun while the patty is cooking.
7. Once cooked, assemble the burger with the patty and bun. Serve hot.

Nutritional Value (Amount per Serving):

Calories: 819; Fat: 50.81; Carb: 40.24; Protein: 51.89

Hawaiian Teriyaki Pork Sandwich

Prep Time: 15 Minutes   Cook Time: 6-7 Minutes   Serves: 1

Ingredients:

- 1/4 pound pork loin, thinly sliced
- 2 tablespoons teriyaki sauce
- 1 pineapple ring (canned or fresh)
- 1 hamburger bun, split

Directions:

1. Preheat Breakfast Sandwich Maker until the green PREHEAT light comes on.
2. Season the sliced pork loin with teriyaki sauce.
3. Place the pork on the bottom ring of the Breakfast Sandwich Maker.
4. Top the pork with a pineapple ring.
5. Close the cover and cook for 6 to 7 minutes until the pork is cooked through.
6. Toast the hamburger bun while the pork is cooking.
7. Once cooked, assemble the sandwich with the pork and bun. Serve hot.

Nutritional Value (Amount per Serving):

Calories: 645; Fat: 28.25; Carb: 48.08; Protein: 48.5

Caramelized Onion and Swiss Patty Melt

Prep Time: 10 Minutes   Cook Time: 8-9 Minutes   Serves: 1

Ingredients:

- 1/4 pound ground beef
- 1/2 cup sliced onions
- 1 slice Swiss cheese
- 2 slices rye bread

Directions:

1. Preheat Breakfast Sandwich Maker until the green PREHEAT light comes on.
2. In a skillet, caramelize the sliced onions.
3. In a bowl, shape ground beef into a patty.
4. Place the patty on the bottom ring of the Breakfast Sandwich Maker.
5. Top the patty with caramelized onions and a slice of Swiss cheese.
6. Close the cover and cook for 8 to 9 minutes until the beef is cooked through.
7. Toast the rye bread while the patty is cooking.
8. Once cooked, assemble the patty melt with the beef and bread. Serve hot.

Nutritional Value (Amount per Serving):

Calories: 905; Fat: 27.77; Carb: 115.3; Protein: 50.27

Pesto Turkey Burger

Prep Time: 12Minutes   Cook Time: 7-8 Minutes   Serves: 1

Ingredients

- 1/4 pound ground turkey
- 1 tablespoon pesto sauce
- 1 slice mozzarella cheese
- 1 hamburger bun, split

Directions:

1. Preheat Breakfast Sandwich Maker until the green PREHEAT light comes on.
2. In a bowl, mix ground turkey with pesto sauce. Shape into a patty.
3. Place the patty on the bottom ring of the Breakfast Sandwich Maker.
4. Top the patty with a slice of mozzarella cheese.
5. Close the cover and cook for 7 to 8 minutes until the turkey is cooked through.
6. Toast the hamburger bun while the patty is cooking.

7. Once cooked, assemble the burger with the patty and bun. Serve hot.

Nutritional Value (Amount per Serving):

Calories: 679; Fat: 39.23; Carb: 37.91; Protein: 45.4

Chili Cheese Dog Sandwich

Prep Time: 10 Minutes   Cook Time: 8-9 Minutes   Serves: 1

Ingredients:

- 1/4 pound beef hot dog
- 1/2 cup chili (canned or homemade)
- 1/4 cup shredded cheddar cheese
- 1 hot dog bun, split

Directions:

1. Preheat Breakfast Sandwich Maker until the green PREHEAT light comes on.
2. Place the beef hot dog on the bottom ring of the Breakfast Sandwich Maker.
3. Spoon chili over the hot dog and sprinkle with shredded cheddar cheese.
4. Close the cover and cook for 8 to 9 minutes until the hot dog is heated through.
5. Toast the hot dog bun while the hot dog is cooking.
6. Once cooked, assemble the sandwich with the hot dog and bun. Serve hot.

Nutritional Value (Amount per Serving):

Calories: 538; Fat: 15.48; Carb: 104.08; Protein: 20.47

Mediterranean Lamb Gyro

Prep Time: 15 Minutes   Cook Time: 7-8 Minutes   Serves: 1

Ingredients:

- 1/4 pound ground lamb
- 1 teaspoon dried oregano
- 1/4 cup diced cucumber
- 1/4 cup diced tomatoes
- 2 tablespoons tzatziki sauce
- 1 pita bread, cut in half

Directions:

1. Preheat Breakfast Sandwich Maker until the green PREHEAT light comes on.
2. In a bowl, mix ground lamb with dried oregano. Shape into a patty.
3. Place the patty on the bottom ring of the Breakfast Sandwich Maker.
4. Close the cover and cook for 7 to 8 minutes until the lamb is cooked through.
5. Meanwhile, prepare the tzatziki sauce.

6. Once cooked, assemble the gyro with the lamb, cucumber, tomatoes, and tzatziki sauce. Serve warm in a pita.

Nutritional Value (Amount per Serving):

Calories: 319; Fat: 14.64; Carb: 20.8; Protein: 26.75

BBQ Brisket Sandwich

Prep Time: 15 Minutes   Cook Time: 10-12 Minutes   Serves: 1

Ingredients:

- 1/4 pound sliced beef brisket
- 2 tablespoons barbecue sauce
- 1/4 cup coleslaw
- 1 hamburger bun, split

Directions:

1. Preheat Breakfast Sandwich Maker until the green PREHEAT light comes on.
2. Place the sliced beef brisket on the bottom ring of the Breakfast Sandwich Maker.
3. Spoon barbecue sauce over the brisket.
4. Close the cover and cook for 10 to 12 minutes until the brisket is heated through.
5. Toast the hamburger bun while the brisket is cooking.
6. Once cooked, assemble the sandwich with the brisket and coleslaw. Serve hot.

Nutritional Value (Amount per Serving):

Calories: 698; Fat: 36.88; Carb: 56.68; Protein: 34.48

Caprese Turkey Burger

Prep Time: 12 Minutes   Cook Time: 7-8 Minutes   Serves: 1

Ingredients:

- 1/4 pound ground turkey
- 1 tablespoon balsamic glaze
- 1 slice fresh mozzarella cheese
- 1 slice tomato
- 1 hamburger bun, split
- Fresh basil leaves

Directions:

1. Preheat Breakfast Sandwich Maker until the green PREHEAT light comes on.
2. In a bowl, mix ground turkey with balsamic glaze. Shape into a patty.
3. Place the patty on the bottom ring of the Breakfast Sandwich Maker.
4. Top the patty with fresh mozzarella cheese and a slice of tomato.

5. Close the cover and cook for 7 to 8 minutes until the turkey is cooked through.
6. Toast the hamburger bun while the patty is cooking.
7. Once cooked, assemble the burger with the patty and bun. Garnish with fresh basil leaves. Serve hot.

Nutritional Value (Amount per Serving):

Calories: 578; Fat: 27.63; Carb: 41.41; Protein: 43.02

Buffalo Chicken Slider

Prep Time: 12 Minutes   Cook Time: 5-6 Minutes   Serves: 1

Ingredients:

- 1/4 pound ground chicken
- 2 tablespoons buffalo sauce
- 1 slider bun, split
- 1 tablespoon ranch dressing
- Lettuce and tomato for garnish

Directions:

1. Preheat Breakfast Sandwich Maker until the green PREHEAT light comes on.
2. In a bowl, mix ground chicken with buffalo sauce. Shape into a small patty.
3. Place the patty on the bottom ring of the Breakfast Sandwich Maker.
4. Close the cover and cook for 5 to 6 minutes until the chicken is cooked through.
5. Toast the slider bun while the patty is cooking.
6. Once cooked, assemble the slider with the patty, ranch dressing, lettuce, and tomato. Serve hot.

Nutritional Value (Amount per Serving):

Calories: 346; Fat: 16.88; Carb: 25.26; Protein: 23.66

Spinach and Feta Stuffed Turkey Burger

Prep Time: 15 Minutes   Cook Time: 7-8 Minutes   Serves: 1

Ingredients:

- 1/4 pound ground turkey
- 1/4 cup chopped spinach
- 2 tablespoons crumbled feta cheese
- 1 hamburger bun, split
- Tzatziki sauce for topping

Directions:

1. Preheat Breakfast Sandwich Maker until the green PREHEAT light comes on.

2. In a bowl, mix ground turkey with chopped spinach and crumbled feta cheese. Shape into a patty.
3. Place the patty on the bottom ring of the Breakfast Sandwich Maker.
4. Close the cover and cook for 7 to 8 minutes until the turkey is cooked through.
5. Toast the hamburger bun while the patty is cooking.
6. Once cooked, assemble the burger with the patty and tzatziki sauce. Serve hot.

Nutritional Value (Amount per Serving):

Calories: 1309; Fat: 88.2; Carb: 48.1; Protein: 82.35

Jalapeño Popper Beef Burger

Prep Time: 12 Minutes   Cook Time: 7-8 Minutes   Serves: 1

Ingredients:

- 1/4 pound ground beef
- 2 tablespoons cream cheese
- 1 tablespoon diced jalapeños
- 1 hamburger bun, split
- Lettuce and tomato for garnish

Directions:

1. Preheat Breakfast Sandwich Maker until the green PREHEAT light comes on.
2. In a bowl, mix ground beef with cream cheese and diced jalapeños. Shape into a patty.
3. Place the patty on the bottom ring of the Breakfast Sandwich Maker.
4. Close the cover and cook for 7 to 8 minutes until the beef is cooked through.
5. Toast the hamburger bun while the patty is cooking.
6. Once cooked, assemble the burger with the patty, lettuce, and tomato. Serve hot.

Nutritional Value (Amount per Serving):

Calories: 734; Fat: 43; Carb: 36.72; Protein: 49.34

Southwest Turkey Club Wrap

Prep Time: 15 Minutes   Cook Time: 5-6 Minutes   Serves: 1

Ingredients:

- 1/4 pound thinly sliced turkey
- 2 slices bacon, cooked and crumbled

- 1/4 cup shredded cheddar cheese
- 1 flour tortilla
- Avocado, lettuce, and tomato for garnish

Directions:

1. Preheat Breakfast Sandwich Maker until the green PREHEAT light comes on.
2. Lay out the flour tortilla on a flat surface.
3. Layer the turkey, bacon, shredded cheddar cheese, avocado, lettuce, and tomato on the tortilla.
4. Roll up the tortilla tightly into a wrap.
5. Place the wrap on the bottom ring of the Breakfast Sandwich Maker and close the cover.
6. Cook for 5 to 6 minutes until the wrap is heated through. Serve warm.

Nutritional Value (Amount per Serving):

Calories: 806; Fat: 59.23; Carb: 31.26; Protein: 36.76

Hawaiian Teriyaki Chicken Burger

Prep Time: 15 Minutes   Cook Time: 6-7 Minutes   Serves: 1

Ingredients:

- 1/4 pound ground chicken
- 2 tablespoons teriyaki sauce
- 1 pineapple ring (canned or fresh)
- 1 hamburger bun, split

Directions:

1. Preheat Breakfast Sandwich Maker until the green PREHEAT light comes on.
2. In a bowl, mix ground chicken with teriyaki sauce. Shape into a patty.
3. Place the patty on the bottom ring of the Breakfast Sandwich Maker.
4. Top the patty with a pineapple ring.
5. Close the cover and cook for 6 to 7 minutes until the chicken is cooked through.
6. Toast the hamburger bun while the patty is cooking.
7. Once cooked, assemble the burger with the patty and bun. Serve hot.

Nutritional Value (Amount per Serving):

Calories: 570; Fat: 24.9; Carb: 48.13; Protein: 39.24

Chapter 3: Fish and Seafood Sandwiches

Grilled Salmon Caesar

Prep Time: 12 Minutes   Cook Time: 6 Minutes   Serves: 1

Ingredients:

- 1 ciabatta roll, sliced
- 1/2 pound grilled salmon fillet
- 2 tablespoons Caesar dressing
- 1 cup chopped romaine lettuce
- 1 tablespoon grated Parmesan cheese
- Salt and pepper to taste
- Lemon wedges for garnish

Directions:

1. Preheat the Breakfast Sandwich Maker until the green PREHEAT light comes on. Lift cover, top ring, and cooking plate.
2. Place bottom half of the ciabatta on the bottom ring
3. Place salmon fillet on the bun.
4. Drizzle Caesar dressing over the salmon.
5. Top with chopped romaine lettuce and Parmesan cheese.
6. Sprinkle with salt and pepper.
7. Lower cooking plate and top ring
8. Cover with the other half of the ciabatta roll.
9. Close cover. Cook for 6 minutes.
10. Slide out the cooking plate, lift cover and rings; garnish with lemon wedges and serve immediately.

Nutritional Value (Amount per Serving):

Calories: 681; Fat: 36.59; Carb: 31.84; Protein: 54.64

Shrimp and Mango Tango

Prep Time: 10 Minutes   Cook Time: 7 Minutes   Serves: 1

Ingredients:

- 1 whole-grain bun, sliced
- 1/2 cup cooked shrimp, peeled and deveined
- 1/4 cup mango salsa
- 2 tablespoons Greek yogurt
- 1 tablespoon chopped cilantro
- Salt and pepper to taste
- Lime wedges for garnish

Directions:

1. Preheat the Breakfast Sandwich Maker until the green PREHEAT light comes on.
2. Mix cooked shrimp with mango salsa, Greek yogurt, chopped cilantro, salt,

and pepper.

3. Place bottom half of the whole-grain bun in the bottom ring
4. Place the mixture on the bottom half of the whole-grain bun.
5. Lower cooking plate and top ring
6. Cover with the other half of the bun.
7. Close cover. Cook for 7 minutes.
8. Slide out the cooking plate, lift cover and rings; garnish with lime wedges and serve immediately.

Nutritional Value (Amount per Serving):

Calories: 707; Fat: 5.48; Carb: 137.27; Protein: 38.86

Tasty Tuna Melt

Prep Time: 8 Minutes   Cook Time: 6 Minutes   Serves: 1

Ingredients:

- 1 English muffin, split
- 1/2 can tuna, drained
- 1/4 cup mayonnaise
- 2 tablespoons diced red onion
- 1/2 cup shredded cheddar cheese
- Salt and pepper to taste
- Fresh parsley for garnish

Directions:

1. Preheat the Breakfast Sandwich Maker until the green PREHEAT light comes on.
2. In a bowl, mix tuna, mayonnaise, diced red onion, salt, and pepper.
3. Place one half of the English muffin in the bottom ring of the Breakfast Sandwich Maker.
4. Spoon the tuna mixture onto one half of the English muffin.
5. Top with shredded cheddar cheese.
6. Cover with the other half of the English muffin.
7. Close cover. Cook for 6 minutes.
8. Slide out the cooking plate, lift cover and rings; garnish with fresh parsley and serve immediately.

Nutritional Value (Amount per Serving):

Calories: 667; Fat: 33.72; Carb: 48.77; Protein: 44.74

Lobster BLT Delight

Prep Time: 15 Minutes   Cook Time: 5 Minutes   Serves: 1

Ingredients:

- 1 pretzel bun, halved

- 1/2 cup cooked lobster meat, chopped
- 2 slices crispy bacon
- 1/2 cup sliced tomatoes
- 1 tablespoon mayonnaise
- Lettuce leaves for garnish
- Salt and pepper to taste

Directions:

1. Preheat the Breakfast Sandwich Maker until the green PREHEAT light comes on.
2. Mix chopped lobster meat with mayonnaise, salt, and pepper.
3. Place the bottom half of the pretzel in the bottom ring.
4. Place the lobster mixture on the bottom half of the pretzel bun.
5. Top with crispy bacon and sliced tomatoes.
6. Lower cooking plate and top ring.
7. Cover with the other half of the pretzel bun.
8. Close cover. Cook for 5 minutes.
9. Slide out the cooking plate, lift cover and rings; garnish with lettuce leaves and serve immediately.

Nutritional Value (Amount per Serving):

Calories: 808; Fat: 30.19; Carb: 102.52; Protein: 34.7

Spicy Tuna Avocado Wrap

Prep Time: 10 Minutes   Cook Time: 8 Minutes   Serves: 1

Ingredients:

- 1 whole-grain wrap
- 1/2 can spicy tuna, drained
- 1/2 avocado, sliced
- 1/4 cup diced cucumber
- 2 tablespoons Sriracha mayo
- Fresh cilantro for garnish
- Salt and pepper to taste

Directions:

1. Preheat the Breakfast Sandwich Maker until the green PREHEAT light comes on.
2. Lay the whole-grain wrap in the Breakfast Sandwich Maker.
3. Spread spicy tuna on one half of the wrap.
4. Arrange avocado slices and diced cucumber over the tuna.
5. Drizzle Sriracha mayo and sprinkle with salt and pepper.
6. Close cover. Cook for 8 minutes.
7. Slide out the cooking plate, lift cover and rings; garnish with fresh cilantro and serve immediately.

Nutritional Value (Amount per Serving):

Calories: 1125; Fat: 31.2; Carb: 179.26; Protein: 49.27

Smoked Trout and Cream Cheese Bagel

Prep Time: 12 Minutes   Cook Time: 5 Minutes   Serves: 1

Ingredients:

- 1 everything bagel, sliced
- 1/2 cup smoked trout
- 2 tablespoons cream cheese
- 1 tablespoon capers
- 1/4 cup red onion slices
- Fresh dill for garnish
- Salt and pepper to taste

Directions:

1. Preheat the Breakfast Sandwich Maker until the green PREHEAT light comes on.
2. Spread cream cheese on the bottom half of the everything bagel and put it in the bottom ring.
3. Arrange smoked trout over the cream cheese.
4. Top with capers and red onion slices.
5. Lower cooking plate and top ring.
6. Cover with the other half of the everything bagel.
7. Close cover. Cook for 5 minutes.
8. Slide out the cooking plate, lift cover and rings; garnish with fresh dill and serve immediately.

Nutritional Value (Amount per Serving):

Calories: 609; Fat: 20.9; Carb: 57.33; Protein: 47.79

Seared Scallop and Mango Salsa Wrap

Prep Time: 15 Minutes   Cook Time: 6 Minutes   Serves: 1

Ingredients:

- 1 spinach tortilla wrap
- 1/2 pound seared scallops
- 1/4 cup mango salsa
- 2 tablespoons Greek yogurt
- 1 cup arugula
- Salt and pepper to taste
- Fresh mint for garnish

Directions:

1. Preheat the Breakfast Sandwich Maker until the green PREHEAT light comes on.
2. Lay the spinach tortilla wrap in the Breakfast Sandwich Maker.

3. Arrange seared scallops on one half of the wrap.
4. Spoon mango salsa over the scallops.
5. Dollop Greek yogurt and top with arugula.
6. Sprinkle with salt and pepper.
7. Close cover. Cook for 6 minutes.
8. Slide out the cooking plate, lift cover and rings; garnish with fresh mint and serve immediately.

Nutritional Value (Amount per Serving):

Calories: 285; Fat: 3.04; Carb: 27.26; Protein: 40.61

Tilapia Tarragon Delight

Prep Time: 12 Minutes   Cook Time: 6 Minutes   Serves: 1

Ingredients:

- 1 brioche bun, sliced
- 1/2 pound tilapia fillet
- 1 tablespoon chopped fresh tarragon
- 1/4 cup cucumber, thinly sliced
- 1 tablespoon lemon zest
- Salt and pepper to taste
- Fresh dill for garnish

Directions:

1. Preheat the Breakfast Sandwich Maker until the green PREHEAT light comes on.
2. Season tilapia fillet with chopped tarragon, salt, and pepper.
3. Place one half of the brioche bun in the bottom ring.
4. Arrange cucumber slices over the fillet and sprinkle with lemon zest.
5. Cover with the other half of the brioche bun.
6. Lower cooking plate and top ring
7. Close cover. Cook for 6 minutes.
8. Slide out the cooking plate, lift cover and rings; garnish with fresh dill and serve immediately.

Nutritional Value (Amount per Serving):

Calories: 695; Fat: 42.72; Carb: 8.25; Protein: 71.3

Crab and Avocado Ciabatta

Prep Time: 10 Minutes   Cook Time: 7 Minutes   Serves: 1

Ingredients:

- 1 ciabatta roll, sliced
- 1/2 cup lump crab meat
- 1/2 avocado, mashed
- 1 tablespoon lime juice

- 1 tablespoon chopped cilantro
- Salt and pepper to taste
- Sliced radishes for garnish

Directions:

1. Preheat the Breakfast Sandwich Maker until the green PREHEAT light comes on.
2. Mix lump crab meat with mashed avocado, lime juice, chopped cilantro, salt, and pepper.
3. Put one half of the ciabatta in the bottom ring.
4. Spread the crab and avocado mixture on the bottom half of the ciabatta roll.
5. Lower cooking plate and top ring.
6. Cover with the other half of the ciabatta roll.
7. Close cover. Cook for 7 minutes.
8. Slide out the cooking plate, lift cover and rings; garnish with sliced radishes and serve immediately.

Nutritional Value (Amount per Serving):

Calories: 437; Fat: 17.73; Carb: 52.1; Protein: 23.92

Lemon Garlic Shrimp Panini

Prep Time: 8 Minutes   Cook Time: 6 Minutes   Serves: 1

Ingredients:

- 1 panini bread, sliced
- 1/2 cup cooked shrimp, peeled and deveined
- 1 tablespoon olive oil
- 1 teaspoon minced garlic
- 1 tablespoon lemon juice
- 1/4 cup baby spinach leaves
- Salt and pepper to taste
- Fresh thyme for garnish

Directions:

1. Preheat the Breakfast Sandwich Maker until the green PREHEAT light comes on.
2. Toss cooked shrimp with olive oil, minced garlic, lemon juice, salt, and pepper.
3. Place one half of the panini bread in the bottom ring.
4. Arrange the shrimp on one half of the panini bread.
5. Top with baby spinach leaves.
6. Lower cooking plate and top ring, and cover with the other half of the panini bread.
7. Close cover. Cook for 6 minutes.
8. Slide out the cooking plate, lift cover and rings; garnish with fresh thyme and serve immediately.

Nutritional Value (Amount per Serving):

Calories: 292; Fat: 15.68; Carb: 23.34; Protein: 17.76

Swordfish and Pineapple Pleasure

Prep Time: 12 Minutes   Cook Time: 6 Minutes   Serves: 1

Ingredients:

- 1 artisanal roll, sliced
- 1/2 pound swordfish steak
- 1/4 cup pineapple salsa
- 1 tablespoon soy sauce
- 1 teaspoon sesame oil
- 1/2 teaspoon ginger, grated
- Salt and pepper to taste
- Chopped green onions for garnish

Directions:

1. Preheat the Breakfast Sandwich Maker until the green PREHEAT light comes on.
2. Rub swordfish steak with soy sauce, sesame oil, grated ginger, salt, and pepper.
3. Place one half of the roll in the bottom ring.
4. Spoon pineapple salsa over the swordfish.
5. Cover with the other half of the artisanal roll.
6. Lower cooking plate and top ring.
7. Close cover. Cook for 6 minutes.
8. Slide out the cooking plate, lift cover and rings; garnish with chopped green onions and serve immediately.

Nutritional Value (Amount per Serving):

Calories: 970; Fat: 49.5; Carb: 64.23; Protein: 65.97

Tarragon Lobster Roll

Prep Time: 15 Minutes   Cook Time: 5 Minutes   Serves: 1

Ingredients:

- 1 split-top roll, sliced
- 1/2 cup cooked lobster meat, chopped
- 2 tablespoons mayonnaise
- 1 tablespoon chopped fresh tarragon
- 1/4 cup celery, finely diced
- Salt and pepper to taste
- Butter lettuce leaves for garnish

Directions:

1. Preheat the Breakfast Sandwich Maker until the green PREHEAT light comes on.
2. Mix chopped lobster meat with mayonnaise, chopped tarragon, diced

celery, salt, and pepper.

3. Fill the split-top roll with the lobster mixture.
4. Garnish with butter lettuce leaves.
5. Slide out the cooking plate, lift cover and rings; serve immediately.

Nutritional Value (Amount per Serving):

Calories: 672; Fat: 34.91; Carb: 67.35; Protein: 25.74

Cajun Catfish Po' Boy

Prep Time: 10 Minutes   Cook Time: 7 Minutes   Serves: 1

Ingredients:

- 1 French baguette, sliced
- 1/2 pound Cajun-seasoned catfish fillet
- 1/4 cup coleslaw
- 2 tablespoons remoulade sauce
- Pickle slices for garnish
- Salt and pepper to taste

Directions:

1. Preheat the Breakfast Sandwich Maker until the green PREHEAT light comes on.
2. Cook Cajun-seasoned catfish fillet in the Breakfast Sandwich Maker.
3. Place the cooked catfish on the sliced French baguette.
4. Top with coleslaw and drizzle with remoulade sauce.
5. Garnish with pickle slices.
6. Close cover. Cook for 7 minutes.
7. Slide out the cooking plate, lift cover and rings; serve immediately.

Nutritional Value (Amount per Serving):

Calories: 1311; Fat: 18.14; Carb: 218.67; Protein: 28.91

Chapter 4: Poultry Sandwiches and Burgers

Sweet and Spicy Turkey Melt

Prep Time: 7 Minutes   Cook Time: 5-6 Minutes   Serves: 1

Ingredients:

- 1 Whole Wheat English Muffin
- 2 slices honey-glazed turkey breast
- 1 tablespoon spicy mustard
- 1 slice Pepper Jack cheese
- 1 large egg, lightly scrambled

Directions:

1. Preheat the Breakfast Sandwich Maker until the green PREHEAT light comes on.
2. Split the Whole Wheat English Muffin in two. Place the bottom half in the bottom ring.
3. Layer with honey-glazed turkey breast, spicy mustard, and Pepper Jack cheese.
4. Lower cooking plate and top ring.
5. Pour the lightly scrambled egg over the cooking plate.
6. Top with the remaining muffin half and cook for 5-6 minutes.
7. Slide out the cooking plate, lift the cover, and rings; carefully remove the sandwich with a spatula.

Nutritional Value (Amount per Serving):

Calories: 346; Fat: 15.59; Carb: 30.14; Protein: 23.11

Turkey Caesar Club Wrap

Prep Time: 8 Minutes   Cook Time: 4-5 Minutes   Serves: 1

Ingredients:

- 1 Light Multi-Grain Flatbread
- 2 slices deli turkey
- 1/4 cup romaine lettuce, shredded
- 2 tablespoons Caesar dressing
- 1 slice Provolone cheese
- 1 large egg, lightly beaten

Directions:

1. Preheat the Breakfast Sandwich Maker until the green PREHEAT light comes on.
2. Lay the Light Multi-Grain Flatbread in the bottom ring.
3. Layer with deli turkey, shredded romaine lettuce, Caesar dressing, and Provolone cheese.
4. Lower cooking plate and top ring
5. Pour the lightly beaten egg over the cooking plate.
6. Fold the flatbread and cook for 4-5 minutes.
7. Slide out the cooking plate, lift the cover, and rings; carefully remove the

wrap with a spatula.

Nutritional Value (Amount per Serving):

Calories: 458; Fat: 32.61; Carb: 13.58; Protein: 27.64

Turkey Ranch BLT

Prep Time: 7 Minutes   Cook Time: 4-5 Minutes   Serves: 1

Ingredients:

- 1 Light Multi-Grain English Muffin
- 2 slices deli turkey
- 2 slices crispy turkey bacon
- 1 tablespoon ranch dressing
- 1 tomato, sliced
- Fresh lettuce leaves

Directions:

1. Preheat the Breakfast Sandwich Maker until the green PREHEAT light comes on.
2. Split the Light Multi-Grain English Muffin in two. Place the bottom half in the bottom ring.
3. Layer with deli turkey, crispy turkey bacon, ranch dressing, tomato slices, and fresh lettuce leaves.
4. Lower cooking plate and top ring.
5. Top with the remaining muffin half and cook for 4-5 minutes.
6. Slide out the cooking plate, lift the cover, and rings; carefully remove the sandwich with a spatula.

Nutritional Value (Amount per Serving):

Calories: 374; Fat: 14.49; Carb: 35.8; Protein: 26.4

Turkey and Cran-Apple Delight

Prep Time: 8 Minutes   Cook Time: 5-6 Minutes   Serves: 1

Ingredients:

- 1 Whole Wheat English Muffin
- 2 slices roasted turkey breast
- 2 tablespoons cran-apple chutney
- 1 slice Gouda cheese
- 1 large egg, lightly beaten

Directions:

1. Preheat the Breakfast Sandwich Maker until the green PREHEAT light comes on.
2. Split the Whole Wheat English Muffin in two. Place the bottom half in the bottom ring.
3. Layer with roasted turkey breast, cran-apple chutney, and Gouda cheese.

4. Lower cooking plate and top ring.
5. Pour the lightly beaten egg over the ingredients.
6. Top with the remaining muffin half and cook for 5-6 minutes.
7. Slide out the cooking plate, lift the cover, and rings; carefully remove the sandwich with a spatula.

Nutritional Value (Amount per Serving):

Calories: 357; Fat: 13.85; Carb: 39.13; Protein: 21.35

Southwest Turkey Wrap

Prep Time: 7 Minutes   Cook Time: 4-5 Minutes   Serves: 1

Ingredients:

- 1 Light Multi-Grain Flatbread
- 2 slices deli turkey
- 1/4 cup black beans, drained and rinsed
- 2 tablespoons salsa
- 1 slice Pepper Jack cheese
- 1 large egg, lightly beaten

Directions:

1. Preheat the Breakfast Sandwich Maker until the green PREHEAT light comes on.
2. Lay the Light Multi-Grain Flatbread in the bottom ring.
3. Layer with deli turkey, black beans, salsa, and Pepper Jack cheese.
4. Lower cooking plate and top ring.
5. Pour the lightly beaten egg over the cooking plate.
6. Fold the flatbread and cook for 4-5 minutes.
7. Slide out the cooking plate, lift the cover, and rings; carefully remove the wrap with a spatula.

Nutritional Value (Amount per Serving):

Calories: 933; Fat: 26.11; Carb: 114.2; Protein: 60.89

Turkey and Guacamole Delight

Prep Time: 8 Minutes   Cook Time: 4-5 Minutes   Serves: 1

Ingredients:

- 1 Light Multi-Grain English Muffin
- 2 slices roasted turkey breast
- 1/4 cup guacamole
- 1 slice Pepper Jack cheese
- 1 large egg, lightly scrambled

Directions:

1. Preheat the Breakfast Sandwich Maker until the green PREHEAT light comes on.
2. Split the Light Multi-Grain English Muffin in two. Place the bottom half in the bottom ring.
3. Layer with roasted turkey breast, guacamole, and Pepper Jack cheese.
4. Lower the cooking plate and top ring.
5. Lower the cooking plate and top ring. Add the lightly scrambled egg.
6. Top with the remaining muffin half and cook for 4-5 minutes.
7. Slide out the cooking plate, lift the cover, and rings; carefully remove the sandwich with a spatula.

Nutritional Value (Amount per Serving):

Calories: 449; Fat: 23.22; Carb: 38.07; Protein: 23.87

Teriyaki Turkey Fusion

Prep Time: 7 Minutes   Cook Time: 5-6 Minutes   Serves: 1

Ingredients:

- 1 Whole Wheat English Muffin
- 2 slices teriyaki turkey breast
- 1 tablespoon teriyaki sauce
- 1 slice Swiss cheese
- 1 large egg, lightly scrambled

Directions:

1. Preheat the Breakfast Sandwich Maker until the green PREHEAT light comes on.
2. Split the Whole Wheat English Muffin in two. Place the bottom half in the bottom ring.
3. Layer with teriyaki turkey breast, teriyaki sauce, and Swiss cheese.
4. Lower the cooking plate and the top ring.
5. Pour the lightly scrambled egg over the cooking plate.
6. Top with the remaining muffin half and cook for 5-6 minutes.
7. Slide out the cooking plate, lift the cover, and rings; carefully remove the sandwich with a spatula.

Nutritional Value (Amount per Serving):

Calories: 347; Fat: 13.82; Carb: 34.82; Protein: 22.32

Turkey and Apple Harvest Wrap

Prep Time: 8 Minutes   Cook Time: 4-5 Minutes   Serves: 1

Ingredients:

- 1 Light Multi-Grain Flatbread
- 2 slices deli turkey
- 1/2 apple, thinly sliced
- 1 tablespoon honey mustard
- 1 slice Cheddar cheese
- 1 large egg, lightly beaten

Directions:

1. Preheat the Breakfast Sandwich Maker until the green PREHEAT light comes on.
2. Lay the Light Multi-Grain Flatbread in the bottom ring.
3. Layer with deli turkey, thinly sliced apple, honey mustard, and Cheddar cheese.
4. Lower the cooking plate and top ring.
5. Pour the lightly beaten egg over the ingredients.
6. Fold the flatbread and cook for 4-5 minutes.
7. Slide out the cooking plate, lift the cover, and rings; carefully remove the wrap with a spatula.

Nutritional Value (Amount per Serving):

Calories: 949; Fat: 27.18; Carb: 120.33; Protein: 56.86

Turkey and Cranberry Panini

Prep Time: 7 Minutes   Cook Time: 5-6 Minutes   Serves: 1

Ingredients:

- 2 slices Whole Grain Bread
- 2 slices roasted turkey breast
- 2 tablespoons cranberry sauce
- 1 slice Brie cheese
- 1 large egg, lightly scrambled

Directions:

1. Preheat the Breakfast Sandwich Maker until the green PREHEAT light comes on.
2. Place one slice of Whole Grain Bread in the bottom ring.
3. Layer with roasted turkey breast, cranberry sauce, and Brie cheese.
4. Lower cooking plate and top ring.
5. Pour the lightly scrambled egg over the ingredients.
6. Top with the remaining bread slice and cook for 5-6 minutes.
7. Slide out the cooking plate, lift the cover, and rings; carefully remove the panini with a spatula.

Nutritional Value (Amount per Serving):

Calories: 467; Fat: 15.95; Carb: 54.34; Protein: 26.47

Turkey and Pesto Panini

Prep Time: 7 Minutes   Cook Time: 5-6 Minutes   Serves: 1

Ingredients:

- 2 slices Italian Ciabatta Bread
- 2 slices roasted turkey breast
- 1 tablespoon pesto sauce
- 1 slice Provolone cheese
- 1 large egg, lightly scrambled

Directions:

1. Preheat the Breakfast Sandwich Maker until the green PREHEAT light comes on.
2. Place one slice of Italian Ciabatta Bread in the bottom ring.
3. Layer with roasted turkey breast, pesto sauce, and Provolone cheese.
4. Lower cooking plate and top ring.
5. Pour the lightly scrambled egg over the cooking plate.
6. Top with the remaining bread slice and cook for 5-6 minutes.
7. Slide out the cooking plate, lift the cover, and rings; carefully remove the panini with a spatula.

Nutritional Value (Amount per Serving):

Calories: 391; Fat: 22.63; Carb: 25.99; Protein: 20.53

Turkey Cran-Orange Wrap

Prep Time: 8 Minutes   Cook Time: 4-5 Minutes   Serves: 1

Ingredients:

- 1 Light Multi-Grain Flatbread
- 2 slices deli turkey
- 2 tablespoons cranberry-orange relish
- 1 slice Swiss cheese
- 1 large egg, lightly beaten

Directions:

1. Preheat the Breakfast Sandwich Maker until the green PREHEAT light comes on.
2. Lay the Light Multi-Grain Flatbread in the bottom ring.
3. Layer with deli turkey, cranberry-orange relish, and Swiss cheese.
4. Lower cooking plate and top ring
5. Pour the lightly beaten egg over the cooking plate.
6. Fold the flatbread and cook for 4-5 minutes.
7. Slide out the cooking plate, lift the cover, and rings; carefully remove the wrap with a spatula.

Nutritional Value (Amount per Serving):

Calories: 921; Fat: 24.59; Carb: 120.26; Protein: 55.36

Turkey and Sun-Dried Tomato Bliss

Prep Time: 7 Minutes   Cook Time: 5-6 Minutes   Serves: 1

Ingredients:

- 1 Light Multi-Grain English Muffin
- 2 slices smoked turkey breast
- 2 tablespoons sun-dried tomato spread
- 1 slice Mozzarella cheese
- 1 large egg, lightly scrambled

Directions:

1. Preheat the Breakfast Sandwich Maker until the green PREHEAT light comes on.
2. Split the Light Multi-Grain English Muffin in two. Place the bottom half in the bottom ring.
3. Layer with smoked turkey breast, sun-dried tomato spread, and Mozzarella cheese.
4. Lower cooking plate and the top ring.
5. Pour the lightly scrambled egg over the cooking plate.
6. Top with the remaining muffin half and cook for 5-6 minutes.
7. Slide out the cooking plate, lift the cover, and rings; carefully remove the sandwich with a spatula.

Nutritional Value (Amount per Serving):

Calories: 351; Fat: 12.71; Carb: 38.83; Protein: 21.25

Turkey and Balsamic Veggie Wrap

Prep Time: 8 Minutes   Cook Time: 4-5 Minutes   Serves: 1

Ingredients:

- 1 Light Multi-Grain Flatbread
- 2 slices deli turkey
- 1/4 cup bell peppers, sliced
- 1 tablespoon balsamic glaze
- 1 slice Provolone cheese
- 1 large egg, lightly beaten

Directions:

1. Preheat the Breakfast Sandwich Maker until the green PREHEAT light comes on.
2. Lay the Light Multi-Grain Flatbread in the bottom ring.

3. Layer with deli turkey, sliced bell peppers, balsamic glaze, and Provolone cheese.
4. Lower cooking plate and the top ring.
5. Pour the lightly beaten egg over the cooking plate.
6. Cover and cook for 4-5 minutes.
7. Slide out the cooking plate, lift the cover, and rings; carefully remove the wrap with a spatula.

Nutritional Value (Amount per Serving):

Calories: 885; Fat: 24.79; Carb: 110.02; Protein: 56.72

Turkey and Applewood Bacon Club

Prep Time: 7 Minutes   Cook Time: 4-5 Minutes   Serves: 1

Ingredients:

- 1 Whole Wheat English Muffin
- 2 slices roasted turkey breast
- 2 slices applewood-smoked bacon, cooked
- 1 tablespoon mayo
- 1 slice Cheddar cheese
- 1 large egg, lightly scrambled

Directions:

1. Preheat the Breakfast Sandwich Maker until the green PREHEAT light comes on.
2. Split the Whole Wheat English Muffin in two. Place the bottom half in the bottom ring.
3. Layer with roasted turkey breast, applewood-smoked bacon, mayo, and Cheddar cheese.
4. Lower cooking plate and the top ring.
5. Pour the lightly scrambled egg over the cooking plate.
6. Top with the remaining muffin half and cook for 4-5 minutes.
7. Slide out the cooking plate, lift the cover, and rings; carefully remove the sandwich with a spatula.

Nutritional Value (Amount per Serving):

Calories: 486; Fat: 28.01; Carb: 31.13; Protein: 28.34

Chapter 5: Vegetarian Sandwiches

Sweet Potato and Kale Morning Delight

Prep Time: 8 Minutes   Cook Time: 4-5 Minutes   Serves: 1

Ingredients:

- 1 English Muffin
- 2 tablespoons pesto
- 1/2 cup sweet potato, grated
- 1/2 cup kale, chopped
- 1 oz. goat cheese
- 1 large egg

Directions:

1. Preheat the Breakfast Sandwich Maker until the green PREHEAT light comes on.
2. Split the English Muffin in two. Spread one half with pesto; set aside.
3. Lift the cover, top ring, and cooking plate. Place half of the English muffin with the pesto side up in the bottom ring. Layer with grated sweet potato, chopped kale, and goat cheese.
4. Lower the cooking plate and top ring. Crack the egg onto the cooking plate. Top with the remaining muffin half, split side down.
5. Close the cover and cook for 4 to 5 minutes.
6. Slide out the cooking plate by rotating the handle clockwise. Lift the cover and rings; carefully remove the sandwich with a plastic spatula.
7. Allow it to cool for a moment, then enjoy.

Nutritional Value (Amount per Serving):

Calories: 493; Fat: 33.52; Carb: 30.29; Protein: 20.23

Raspberry Almond Crunch Delight

Prep Time: 7 Minutes   Cook Time: 4-5 Minutes   Serves: 1

Ingredients:

- 1 English Muffin
- 2 tablespoons almond butter
- 1/4 cup fresh raspberries
- 1 tablespoon sliced almonds
- 1 tablespoon honey
- 1 large egg

Directions:

1. Preheat the Breakfast Sandwich Maker until the green PREHEAT light comes on.
2. Split the English Muffin in two. Spread one half with almond butter; set aside.
3. Lift the cover, top ring, and cooking plate. Place half of the English muffin with the almond butter side up in the bottom ring. Layer with fresh raspberries, sliced almonds, and drizzle honey.
4. Lower the cooking plate and top ring. Crack the egg onto the cooking plate.

Top with the remaining muffin half, split side down.

5. Close the cover and cook for 4 to 5 minutes.
6. Slide out the cooking plate by rotating the handle clockwise. Lift the cover and rings; carefully remove the sandwich with a plastic spatula.
7. Allow it to cool for a moment, then indulge in your Raspberry Almond Crunch Delight!

Nutritional Value (Amount per Serving):

Calories: 507; Fat: 24.09; Carb: 64.68; Protein: 15.21

Southwest Spinach and Black Bean Fiesta

Prep Time: 9 Minutes   Cook Time: 4-5 Minutes   Serves: 1

Ingredients:

- 1 English Muffin
- 2 tablespoons salsa
- 1/2 cup fresh spinach leaves
- 1/4 cup black beans, mashed
- 1 oz. shredded Monterey Jack cheese
- 1 large egg

Directions:

1. Preheat the Breakfast Sandwich Maker until the green PREHEAT light comes on.
2. Split the English Muffin in two. Spread one half with salsa; set aside.
3. Lift the cover, top ring, and cooking plate. Place half of the English muffin with the salsa side up in the bottom ring. Layer with fresh spinach leaves, mashed black beans, and shredded Monterey Jack cheese.
4. Lower the cooking plate and top ring. Crack the egg onto the cooking plate. Top with the remaining muffin half, split side down.
5. Close the cover and cook for 4 to 5 minutes.
6. Slide out the cooking plate by rotating the handle clockwise. Lift the cover and rings; carefully remove the sandwich with a plastic spatula.
7. Allow it to cool for a moment, then enjoy!

Nutritional Value (Amount per Serving):

Calories: 467; Fat: 15.06; Carb: 59.55; Protein: 26.07

Mango Avocado Salsa Morning Delight

Prep Time: 8 Minutes   Cook Time: 4-5 Minutes   Serves: 1

Ingredients:

- 1 English Muffin
- 1/2 ripe avocado, mashed

- 1/4 cup mango, diced
- 1 tablespoon red onion, finely chopped
- 1 tablespoon cilantro, chopped
- 1 large egg

Directions:

1. Preheat the Breakfast Sandwich Maker until the green PREHEAT light comes on.
2. Split the English Muffin in two. Spread one half with mashed avocado; set aside.
3. Lift the cover, top ring, and cooking plate. Place half of the English muffin with the avocado side up in the bottom ring. Combine mango, red onion, and cilantro to create a salsa, then layer on top of the avocado.
4. Lower the cooking plate and top ring. Crack the egg onto the cooking plate. Top with the remaining muffin half, split side down.
5. Close the cover and cook for 4 to 5 minutes.
6. Slide out the cooking plate by rotating the handle clockwise. Lift the cover and rings; carefully remove the sandwich with a plastic spatula.
7. Allow it to cool for a moment, then savor your Mango Avocado Salsa Morning Delight!

Nutritional Value (Amount per Serving):

Calories: 372; Fat: 20.56; Carb: 41.93; Protein: 10.14

Mediterranean Roasted Red Pepper Hummus Delight

Prep Time: 7 Minutes   Cook Time: 4-5 Minutes   Serves: 1

Ingredients:

- 1 English Muffin
- 2 tablespoons roasted red pepper hummus
- 1/4 cup cherry tomatoes, halved
- 1/4 cup cucumber, diced
- 1 oz. crumbled feta cheese
- 1 large egg

Directions:

1. Preheat the Breakfast Sandwich Maker until the green PREHEAT light comes on.
2. Split the English Muffin in two. Spread one half with roasted red pepper hummus; set aside.
3. Lift the cover, top ring, and cooking plate. Place half of the English muffin with the hummus side up in the bottom ring. Layer with halved cherry tomatoes, diced cucumber, and crumbled feta cheese.
4. Lower the cooking plate and top ring. Crack the egg onto the cooking plate.

Top with the remaining muffin half, split side down.

5. Close the cover and cook for 4 to 5 minutes.
6. Slide out the cooking plate by rotating the handle clockwise. Lift the cover and rings; carefully remove the sandwich with a plastic spatula.
7. Allow it to cool for a moment, then enjoy!

Nutritional Value (Amount per Serving):

Calories: 271; Fat: 11.95; Carb: 30.06; Protein: 12.16

Apple Cinnamon Crunch Morning Delight

Prep Time: 8 Minutes   Cook Time: 4-5 Minutes   Serves: 1

Ingredients:

- 1 English Muffin
- 2 tablespoons cream cheese
- 1/4 cup apple, thinly sliced
- 1 tablespoon brown sugar
- 1 tablespoon chopped walnuts
- 1 large egg

Directions:

1. Preheat the Breakfast Sandwich Maker until the green PREHEAT light comes on.
2. Split the English Muffin in two. Spread one half with cream cheese; set aside.
3. Lift the cover, top ring, and cooking plate. Place half of the English muffin with the cream cheese side up in the bottom ring. Layer with thinly sliced apples, brown sugar, and chopped walnuts.
4. Lower the cooking plate and top ring. Crack the egg onto the cooking plate. Top with the remaining muffin half, split side down.
5. Close the cover and cook for 4 to 5 minutes.
6. Slide out the cooking plate by rotating the handle clockwise. Lift the cover and rings; carefully remove the sandwich with a plastic spatula.
7. Allow it to cool for a moment, then indulge in your Apple Cinnamon Crunch Morning Delight!

Nutritional Value (Amount per Serving):

Calories: 360; Fat: 18.91; Carb: 38.68; Protein: 11.74

Caprese Avocado Morning Bliss

Prep Time: 6 Minutes   Cook Time: 4-5 Minutes   Serves: 1

Ingredients:

- 1 English Muffin
- 1/2 ripe avocado, sliced

- 1 oz. fresh mozzarella, sliced
- 1 small tomato, thinly sliced
- Fresh basil leaves
- 1 large egg

Directions:

1. Preheat the Breakfast Sandwich Maker until the green PREHEAT light comes on.
2. Split the English Muffin in two. Place half of the English muffin with the avocado side up in the bottom ring.
3. Layer with sliced avocado, fresh mozzarella, tomato slices, and fresh basil leaves.
4. Lower the cooking plate and top ring. Crack the egg onto the cooking plate. Top with the remaining muffin half, split side down.
5. Close the cover and cook for 4 to 5 minutes.
6. Slide out the cooking plate by rotating the handle clockwise. Lift the cover and rings; carefully remove the sandwich with a plastic spatula.
7. Allow it to cool for a moment, then enjoy.

Nutritional Value (Amount per Serving):

Calories: 386; Fat: 20.42; Carb: 36.31; Protein: 18.82

Greek Salad Morning Delight

Prep Time: 7 Minutes   Cook Time: 4-5 Minutes   Serves: 1

Ingredients:

- 1 English Muffin
- 2 tablespoons tzatziki sauce
- 1/4 cup cucumber, diced
- 1/4 cup cherry tomatoes, halved
- 1/4 cup Kalamata olives, sliced
- 1 oz. crumbled feta cheese
- 1 large egg

Directions:

1. Preheat the Breakfast Sandwich Maker until the green PREHEAT light comes on.
2. Split the English Muffin in two. Spread one half with tzatziki sauce; set aside.
3. Lift the cover, top ring, and cooking plate. Place half of the English muffin with the tzatziki side up in the bottom ring. Layer with diced cucumber, halved cherry tomatoes, sliced Kalamata olives, and crumbled feta cheese.
4. Lower the cooking plate and top ring. Crack the egg onto the cooking plate. Top with the remaining muffin half, split side down.
5. Close the cover and cook for 4 to 5 minutes.
6. Slide out the cooking plate by rotating the handle clockwise. Lift the cover and rings; carefully remove the sandwich with a plastic spatula.
7. Allow it to cool for a moment, then enjoy.

Nutritional Value (Amount per Serving):

Calories: 311; Fat: 15.4; Carb: 32.81; Protein: 12.73

Pineapple Coconut Morning Bliss

Prep Time: 8 Minutes   Cook Time: 4-5 Minutes   Serves: 1

Ingredients:

- 1 English Muffin
- 2 tablespoons coconut cream
- 1/4 cup pineapple, diced
- 1 tablespoon shredded coconut
- 1 tablespoon chopped macadamia nuts
- 1 large egg

Directions:

1. Preheat the Breakfast Sandwich Maker until the green PREHEAT light comes on.
2. Split the English Muffin in two. Spread one half with coconut cream; set aside.
3. Lift the cover, top ring, and cooking plate. Place half of the English muffin with the coconut cream side up in the bottom ring. Layer with diced pineapple, shredded coconut, and chopped macadamia nuts.
4. Lower the cooking plate and top ring. Crack the egg onto the cooking plate. Top with the remaining muffin half, split side down.
5. Close the cover and cook for 4 to 5 minutes.
6. Slide out the cooking plate by rotating the handle clockwise. Lift the cover and rings; carefully remove the sandwich with a plastic spatula.
7. Allow it to cool for a moment, then indulge in your Pineapple Coconut Morning Bliss!

Nutritional Value (Amount per Serving):

Calories: 372; Fat: 21.52; Carb: 39.46; Protein: 9.68

Mediterranean Eggplant Delight

Prep Time: 10 Minutes   Cook Time: 4-5 Minutes   Serves: 1

Ingredients:

- 1 English Muffin
- 2 tablespoons tzatziki sauce
- 1/2 cup grilled eggplant, sliced
- 1/4 cup cherry tomatoes, halved
- 1/4 cup cucumber, diced
- 1 oz. crumbled feta cheese

- 1 large egg

Directions:

1. Preheat the Breakfast Sandwich Maker until the green PREHEAT light comes on.
2. Split the English Muffin in two. Spread one half with tzatziki sauce; set aside.
3. Lift the cover, top ring, and cooking plate. Place half of the English muffin with the tzatziki side up in the bottom ring. Layer with grilled eggplant, halved cherry tomatoes, diced cucumber, and crumbled feta cheese.
4. Lower the cooking plate and top ring. Crack the egg onto the cooking plate. Top with the remaining muffin half, split side down.
5. Close the cover and cook for 4 to 5 minutes.
6. Slide out the cooking plate by rotating the handle clockwise. Lift the cover and rings; carefully remove the sandwich with a plastic spatula.
7. Allow it to cool for a moment, then enjoy.

Nutritional Value (Amount per Serving):

Calories: 289; Fat: 11.92; Carb: 35.03; Protein: 12.85

Blueberry Almond Cream Cheese Bliss

Prep Time: 7 Minutes   Cook Time: 4-5 Minutes   Serves: 1

Ingredients:

- 1 English Muffin
- 2 tablespoons almond butter
- 2 tablespoons cream cheese
- 1/4 cup fresh blueberries
- 1 tablespoon sliced almonds
- 1 large egg

Directions:

1. Preheat the Breakfast Sandwich Maker until the green PREHEAT light comes on.
2. Split the English Muffin in two. Spread one half with almond butter, and the other half with cream cheese; set aside.
3. Lift the cover, top ring, and cooking plate. Place half of the English muffin with the almond butter side up in the bottom ring. Layer with fresh blueberries and sliced almonds.
4. Lower the cooking plate and top ring. Crack the egg onto the cooking plate. Top with the remaining muffin half, split side down.
5. Close the cover and cook for 4 to 5 minutes.
6. Slide out the cooking plate by rotating the handle clockwise. Lift the cover and rings; carefully remove the sandwich with a plastic spatula.
7. Allow it to cool for a moment, then indulge in your Blueberry Almond Cream Cheese Bliss!

Nutritional Value (Amount per Serving):

Calories: 530; Fat: 32.8; Carb: 47.6; Protein: 17.16

Southwest Avocado Black Bean Fiesta

Prep Time: 9 Minutes   Cook Time: 4-5 Minutes   Serves: 1

Ingredients:

- 1 English Muffin
- 2 tablespoons salsa
- 1/2 ripe avocado, mashed
- 1/4 cup black beans, drained and
- rinsed
- 1 oz. shredded cheddar cheese
- 1 large egg

Directions:

1. Preheat the Breakfast Sandwich Maker until the green PREHEAT light comes on.
2. Split the English Muffin in two. Spread one half with salsa; set aside.
3. Lift the cover, top ring, and cooking plate. Place half of the English muffin with the salsa side up in the bottom ring. Layer with mashed avocado, black beans, and shredded cheddar cheese.
4. Lower the cooking plate and top ring. Crack the egg onto the cooking plate. Top with the remaining muffin half, split side down.
5. Close the cover and cook for 4 to 5 minutes.
6. Slide out the cooking plate by rotating the handle clockwise. Lift the cover and rings; carefully remove the sandwich with a plastic spatula.
7. Allow it to cool for a moment, then enjoy.

Nutritional Value (Amount per Serving):

Calories: 460; Fat: 23.2; Carb: 50.38; Protein: 17.84

Banana Nutella Crunch Morning Delight

Prep Time: 7 Minutes   Cook Time: 4-5 Minutes   Serves: 1

Ingredients:

- 1 English Muffin
- 2 tablespoons Nutella
- 1 banana, thinly sliced
- 1 tablespoon chopped hazelnuts
- 1 large egg

Directions:

1. Preheat the Breakfast Sandwich Maker until the green PREHEAT light comes on.
2. Split the English Muffin in two. Spread one half with Nutella; set aside.

3. Lift the cover, top ring, and cooking plate. Place half of the English muffin with the Nutella side up in the bottom ring. Layer with thinly sliced bananas and chopped hazelnuts.
4. Lower the cooking plate and top ring. Crack the egg onto the cooking plate. Top with the remaining muffin half, split side down.
5. Close the cover and cook for 4 to 5 minutes.
6. Slide out the cooking plate by rotating the handle clockwise. Lift the cover and rings; carefully remove the sandwich with a plastic spatula.
7. Allow it to cool for a moment, then indulge in your Banana Nutella Crunch Morning Delight!

Nutritional Value (Amount per Serving):

Calories: 1599; Fat: 99.05; Carb: 166.48; Protein: 32.16

Spinach and Sun-Dried Tomato Morning Delight

Prep Time: 8 Minutes   Cook Time: 4-5 Minutes   Serves: 1

Ingredients:

- 1 English Muffin
- 2 tablespoons cream cheese
- 1/2 cup fresh spinach leaves
- 2 tablespoons sun-dried tomatoes, chopped
- 1 oz. feta cheese, crumbled
- 1 large egg

Directions:

1. Preheat the Breakfast Sandwich Maker until the green PREHEAT light comes on.
2. Split the English Muffin in two. Spread one half with cream cheese; set aside.
3. Lift the cover, top ring, and cooking plate. Place half of the English muffin with the cream cheese side up in the bottom ring. Layer with fresh spinach leaves, chopped sun-dried tomatoes, and crumbled feta cheese.
4. Lower the cooking plate and top ring. Crack the egg onto the cooking plate. Top with the remaining muffin half, split side down.
5. Close the cover and cook for 4 to 5 minutes.
6. Slide out the cooking plate by rotating the handle clockwise. Lift the cover and rings; carefully remove the sandwich with a plastic spatula.
7. Allow it to cool for a moment, then enjoy.

Nutritional Value (Amount per Serving):

Calories: 366; Fat: 20.54; Carb: 32.69; Protein: 15.21

Chapter 6: Eggs Sandwiches

Southwest Breakfast Burrito

Prep Time: 8 Minutes   Cook Time: 4 Minutes   Serves: 1

Ingredients:

- 1 large flour tortilla
- 1/4 cup black beans, drained and rinsed
- 2 tablespoons salsa
- 1 large egg
- 1/4 cup shredded cheddar cheese
- Fresh cilantro for garnish

Directions:

1. Preheat the Breakfast Sandwich Maker until the green PREHEAT light comes on.
2. Lay the flour tortilla flat.
3. Spread black beans and salsa over one half of the tortilla.
4. Lift the cover, top ring, and cooking plate. Place the bean and salsa-covered tortilla in the bottom ring.
5. Lower cooking plate and top ring.Add a cracked egg on top of cooking plate.
6. Close the cover and cook for 3 to 4 minutes or until the egg is cooked through.
7. Assemble the burrito, garnish with fresh cilantro, and enjoy the Southwest breakfast goodness!

Nutritional Value (Amount per Serving):

Calories: 363; Fat: 12.67; Carb: 43.87; Protein: 18.69

Greek Yogurt Parfait Wrap

Prep Time: 7 Minutes   Cook Time: 3 Minutes   Serves: 1

Ingredients:

- 1 whole wheat wrap
- 2 tablespoons Greek yogurt
- 1/4 cup granola
- 1/4 cup mixed berries (strawberries, blueberries, raspberries)
- 1 large egg
- Honey for drizzling

Directions:

1. Preheat the Breakfast Sandwich Maker until the green PREHEAT light comes on.
2. Lay the whole wheat wrap flat.
3. Spread Greek yogurt over the entire surface of the wrap.

4. Lift the cover, top ring, and cooking plate. Place the yogurt-covered wrap in the bottom ring.
5. Sprinkle granola and mixed berries on top.
6. Lower the cooking plate and top ring. Add a cracked egg to the cooking plate.
7. Close the cover and cook for 2 to 3 minutes or until the egg is cooked to your liking.
8. Assemble the wrap, drizzle with honey, and enjoy.

Nutritional Value (Amount per Serving):

Calories: 834; Fat: 31.3; Carb: 120.36; Protein: 23.15

California Veggie Delight

Prep Time: 6 Minutes   Cook Time: 3 Minutes   Serves: 1

Ingredients:

- 1 whole grain English muffin
- 2 tablespoons guacamole
- 1 slice tomato
- 1/4 cup alfalfa sprouts
- 1 large egg
- Salt and pepper to taste

Directions:

1. Preheat the Breakfast Sandwich Maker until the green PREHEAT light comes on.
2. Split and lightly toast the whole grain English muffin.
3. Spread guacamole on one half of the muffin.
4. Lift the cover, top ring, and cooking plate. Place the guacamole-covered muffin in the bottom ring.
5. Add a slice of tomato and a generous portion of alfalfa sprouts.
6. Lower the cooking plate and top ring. Add a cracked egg to the cooking plate.
7. Season the egg with salt and pepper to taste. Close the cover and cook for 2 to 3 minutes or until the egg is cooked through.
8. Assemble the sandwich and enjoy!

Nutritional Value (Amount per Serving):

Calories: 255; Fat: 7.91; Carb: 37.39; Protein: 10.34

Tex-Mex Fiesta Wrap

Prep Time: 8 Minutes   Cook Time: 4 Minutes   Serves: 1

Ingredients:

- 1 spinach wrap

- 2 tablespoons black bean dip
- 1/4 cup corn kernels
- 1/4 cup diced tomatoes
- 1 large egg
- 1 tablespoon shredded Mexican blend cheese
- Fresh cilantro for garnish

Directions:

1. Preheat the Breakfast Sandwich Maker until the green PREHEAT light comes on.
2. Lay the spinach wrap flat.
3. Spread black bean dip over the entire surface of the wrap.
4. Lift the cover, top ring, and cooking plate. Place the bean dip-covered wrap in the bottom ring.
5. Add corn kernels and diced tomatoes on top.
6. Lower the cooking plate and top ring. Add a cracked egg to the cooking plate.
7. Sprinkle shredded Mexican blend cheese on the egg. Close the cover and cook for 3 to 4 minutes or until the egg is cooked through.
8. Assemble the wrap, garnish with fresh cilantro, and indulge in the Tex-Mex fiesta!

Nutritional Value (Amount per Serving):

Calories: 180; Fat: 7.67; Carb: 19.61; Protein: 13.24

Mushroom and Swiss Sunrise

Prep Time: 5 Minutes   Cook Time: 2 Minutes   Serves: 1

Ingredients:

- 1 croissant, sliced in half
- 2 tablespoons garlic aioli
- 1/2 cup sliced mushrooms, sautéed
- 1 slice Swiss cheese
- 1 large egg
- Salt and pepper to taste

Directions:

1. Preheat the Breakfast Sandwich Maker until the green PREHEAT light comes on.
2. Slice the croissant in half.
3. Spread garlic aioli on one half of the croissant.
4. Lift the cover, top ring, and cooking plate. Place the aioli-covered croissant in the bottom ring.
5. Layer sautéed mushrooms and a slice of Swiss cheese on top.
6. Lower the cooking plate and top ring. Add a cracked egg to the cooking plate.

7. Season the egg with salt and pepper to taste. Close the cover and cook for 1 to 2 minutes or until the egg is cooked through.
8. Assemble the sandwich and enjoy!

Nutritional Value (Amount per Serving):

Calories: 371; Fat: 20.69; Carb: 33.29; Protein: 14.21

Apple Cinnamon Breakfast Delight

Prep Time: 6 Minutes   Cook Time: 3 Minutes   Serves: 1

Ingredients:

- 1 cinnamon raisin bagel, sliced and toasted
- 2 tablespoons cream cheese
- 1/2 apple, thinly sliced
- 1 large egg
- Ground cinnamon for sprinkling
- Maple syrup for drizzling

Directions:

1. Preheat the Breakfast Sandwich Maker until the green PREHEAT light comes on.
2. Slice and toast the cinnamon raisin bagel.
3. Spread cream cheese on one half of the bagel.
4. Lift the cover, top ring, and cooking plate. Place the cream cheese-covered bagel in the bottom ring.
5. Arrange thinly sliced apples on top.
6. Lower the cooking plate and top ring. Add a cracked egg to the cooking plate.
7. Sprinkle ground cinnamon on the egg. Close the cover and cook for 2 to 3 minutes or until the egg is cooked to your liking.
8. Assemble the sandwich, drizzle with maple syrup, and savor the apple cinnamon breakfast delight!

Nutritional Value (Amount per Serving):

Calories: 498; Fat: 15.05; Carb: 77.42; Protein: 15.04

Caprese English Muffin Melt

Prep Time: 5 Minutes   Cook Time: 2 Minutes   Serves: 1

Ingredients:

- 1 whole grain English muffin, sliced and toasted

- 2 tablespoons balsamic glaze
- 1 slice mozzarella cheese
- 1 slice tomato
- Fresh basil leaves
- 1 large egg
- Salt and pepper to taste

Directions:

1. Preheat the Breakfast Sandwich Maker until the green PREHEAT light comes on.
2. Split and lightly toast the whole grain English muffin.
3. Drizzle balsamic glaze on one half of the muffin.
4. Lift the cover, top ring, and cooking plate. Place the balsamic-glazed muffin in the bottom ring.
5. Add a slice of mozzarella cheese and a slice of tomato.
6. Sprinkle fresh basil leaves on top.
7. Lower the cooking plate and top ring. Add a cracked egg to the cooking plate.
8. Season the egg with salt and pepper to taste. Close the cover and cook for 1 to 2 minutes or until the egg is cooked through.
9. Assemble the sandwich and enjoy!

Nutritional Value (Amount per Serving):

Calories: 313; Fat: 9.3; Carb: 46.25; Protein: 14.45

Blueberry Almond Morning Wrap

Prep Time: 7 Minutes   Cook Time: 3 Minutes   Serves: 1

Ingredients:

- 1 whole wheat wrap
- 2 tablespoons almond butter
- 1/4 cup fresh blueberries
- 1 tablespoon sliced almonds
- 1 large egg
- Honey for drizzling

Directions:

1. Preheat the Breakfast Sandwich Maker until the green PREHEAT light comes on.
2. Lay the whole wheat wrap flat.
3. Spread almond butter over the entire surface of the wrap.
4. Lift the cover, top ring, and cooking plate. Place the almond butter-covered wrap in the bottom ring.
5. Sprinkle fresh blueberries and sliced almonds on top.
6. Lower the cooking plate and top ring. Add a cracked egg to the cooking plate.

7. Close the cover and cook for 2 to 3 minutes or until the egg is cooked to your liking.
8. Assemble the wrap, drizzle with honey, and enjoy!

Nutritional Value (Amount per Serving):

Calories: 617; Fat: 24.31; Carb: 87.05; Protein: 22.18

Turkey Pesto Morning Delight

Prep Time: 6 Minutes   Cook Time: 3 Minutes   Serves: 1

Ingredients:

- 1 multigrain English muffin, sliced and toasted
- 2 tablespoons pesto sauce
- 2 slices deli turkey
- 1 slice provolone cheese
- 1 large egg
- Salt and pepper to taste
- Fresh spinach leaves for garnish

Directions:

1. Preheat the Breakfast Sandwich Maker until the green PREHEAT light comes on.
2. Slice and toast the multigrain English muffin.
3. Spread pesto sauce on one half of the muffin.
4. Lift the cover, top ring, and cooking plate. Place the pesto-covered muffin in the bottom ring.
5. Layer deli turkey slices and a slice of provolone cheese on top.
6. Lower the cooking plate and top ring. Add a cracked egg to the cooking plate.
7. Season the egg with salt and pepper to taste. Close the cover and cook for 2 to 3 minutes or until the egg is cooked through.
8. Assemble the sandwich, garnish with fresh spinach leaves, and enjoy!

Nutritional Value (Amount per Serving):

Calories: 578; Fat: 33.8; Carb: 37.45; Protein: 34.28

Sweet Potato and Kale Breakfast Wrap

Prep Time: 8 Minutes   Cook Time: 4 Minutes   Serves: 1

Ingredients:

- 1 whole wheat wrap

- 1/2 cup sweet potato, grated and sautéed
- Handful of kale, chopped and sautéed
- 1 large egg
- Salt and pepper to taste
- Feta cheese for extra flavor

Directions:

1. Preheat the Breakfast Sandwich Maker until the green PREHEAT light comes on.
2. Lay the whole wheat wrap flat.
3. Sauté grated sweet potato until tender and spread it on the wrap.
4. Sauté chopped kale until wilted and add it on top.
5. Lift the cover, top ring, and cooking plate. Place the sweet potato and kale-covered wrap in the bottom ring.
6. Lower the cooking plate and top ring. Add a cracked egg to the cooking plate.
7. Season the egg with salt and pepper to taste. Close the cover and cook for 3 to 4 minutes or until the egg is cooked through.
8. Assemble the wrap, sprinkle feta cheese for extra flavor, and enjoy!

Nutritional Value (Amount per Serving):

Calories: 416; Fat: 9.19; Carb: 70.33; Protein: 19.67

Chicken and Waffle Breakfast Stack

Prep Time: 10 Minutes   Cook Time: 5 Minutes   Serves: 1

Ingredients:

- 2 frozen mini waffles
- 1/2 cup shredded rotisserie chicken
- 1 large egg
- Salt and pepper to taste
- Maple syrup for drizzling

Directions:

1. Preheat the Breakfast Sandwich Maker until the green PREHEAT light comes on.
2. Toast the frozen mini waffles until golden brown.
3. Place one waffle in the bottom ring of the maker.
4. Layer shredded rotisserie chicken on top of the waffle.
5. Lower the cooking plate and top ring. Add a cracked egg to the cooking plate.
6. Season the egg with salt and pepper to taste. Close the cover and cook for 3 to 4 minutes or until the egg is cooked through.
7. Place the second toasted waffle on top, drizzle with maple syrup, and enjoy!

Nutritional Value (Amount per Serving):

Calories: 539; Fat: 22.27; Carb: 39.84; Protein: 45.52

Tomato Basil Bagel Bliss

Prep Time: 6 Minutes   Cook Time: 3 Minutes   Serves: 1

Ingredients:

- 1 plain bagel, sliced and toasted
- 2 tablespoons cream cheese
- 1 slice tomato
- Fresh basil leaves
- 1 large egg
- Salt and pepper to taste

Directions:

1. Preheat the Breakfast Sandwich Maker until the green PREHEAT light comes on.
2. Slice and toast the plain bagel.
3. Spread cream cheese on one half of the bagel.
4. Lift the cover, top ring, and cooking plate. Place the cream cheese-covered bagel in the bottom ring.
5. Add a slice of tomato and fresh basil leaves.
6. Lower the cooking plate and top ring. Add a cracked egg to the cooking plate.
7. Season the egg with salt and pepper to taste. Close the cover and cook for 2 to 3 minutes or until the egg is cooked through.
8. Assemble the sandwich and savor the tomato basil bagel bliss!

Nutritional Value (Amount per Serving):

Calories: 425; Fat: 14.52; Carb: 58.37; Protein: 16.33

Chapter 7: Fruit Sandwiches

Blueberry Bliss Breakfast Sandwich

Prep Time: 10 Minutes   Cook Time: 3-4 Minutes   Serves: 1

Ingredients:

- 2 tablespoons whipped cream cheese
- 1 tablespoon blueberry jam
- 1/2 cup fresh blueberries
- 1 tablespoon sliced almonds
- 2 teaspoons unsalted butter, at room temperature
- 2 slices blueberry swirl bread, cut into 4-inch circles

Directions:

1. Combine whipped cream cheese and blueberry jam in a small bowl.
2. Preheat Breakfast Sandwich Maker until the green PREHEAT light comes on. Lift cover, top ring, and cooking plate.
3. Spread 1 teaspoon butter on one side of each blueberry swirl bread circle.
4. Flip bread circles over and spread 1 tablespoon of the cream cheese mixture on each slice.
5. Place one circle of blueberry swirl bread onto the bottom plate, buttered side down. Top with fresh blueberries and sliced almonds.
6. Lower the top ring and cooking plate. Add the remaining blueberries and bread, buttered side up.
7. Close cover and cook for 3 to 4 minutes.
8. Slide out the cooking plate by rotating the handle clockwise. Lift cover and rings; carefully remove the sandwich with a plastic spatula.

Nutritional Value (Amount per Serving):

Calories: 393; Fat: 15.25; Carb: 64.36; Protein: 4.55

Raspberry Rhapsody Breakfast Sandwich

Prep Time: 12 Minutes   Cook Time: 3-4 Minutes   Serves: 1

Ingredients:

- 2 tablespoons raspberry-flavored cream cheese
- 1 tablespoon raspberry preserves
- 1/2 cup fresh raspberries
- 1 tablespoon crushed graham crackers
- 2 teaspoons unsalted butter, at room temperature
- 2 slices raspberry swirl bread, cut into 4-inch circles

Directions:

1. Mix raspberry-flavored cream cheese and raspberry preserves in a small

bowl.

2. Preheat Breakfast Sandwich Maker until the green PREHEAT light comes on. Lift cover, top ring, and cooking plate.
3. Spread 1 teaspoon butter on one side of each raspberry swirl bread circle.
4. Flip bread circles over and spread 1 tablespoon of the cream cheese mixture on each slice.
5. Place one circle of raspberry swirl bread onto the bottom plate, buttered side down. Top with fresh raspberries and crushed graham crackers.
6. Lower the top ring and cooking plate. Add the remaining raspberries and bread, buttered side up.
7. Close cover and cook for 3 to 4 minutes.
8. Slide out the cooking plate by rotating the handle clockwise. Lift cover and rings; carefully remove the sandwich with a plastic spatula.

Nutritional Value (Amount per Serving):

Calories: 332; Fat: 15.49; Carb: 46.79; Protein: 4.68

Pineapple Paradise Breakfast Sandwich

Prep Time: 15 Minutes   Cook Time: 3-4 Minutes   Serves: 1

Ingredients:

- 2 tablespoons coconut-flavored Greek yogurt
- 1 tablespoon pineapple preserves
- 1/2 cup pineapple chunks
- 1 tablespoon toasted coconut flakes
- 2 teaspoons unsalted butter, at room temperature
- 2 slices pineapple bread, cut into 4-inch circles

Directions:

1. Combine coconut-flavored Greek yogurt and pineapple preserves in a small bowl.
2. Preheat Breakfast Sandwich Maker until the green PREHEAT light comes on. Lift cover, top ring, and cooking plate.
3. Spread 1 teaspoon butter on one side of each pineapple bread circle.
4. Flip bread circles over and spread 1 tablespoon of the yogurt mixture on each slice.
5. Place one circle of pineapple bread onto the bottom plate, buttered side down. Top with pineapple chunks and toasted coconut flakes.
6. Lower the top ring and cooking plate. Add the remaining pineapple chunks and bread, buttered side up.
7. Close cover and cook for 3 to 4 minutes.
8. Slide out the cooking plate by rotating the handle clockwise. Lift cover and

rings; carefully remove the sandwich with a plastic spatula.

Nutritional Value (Amount per Serving):

Calories: 259; Fat: 7.82; Carb: 48.13; Protein: 2.48

Strawberry Fields Breakfast Sandwich

Prep Time: 12 Minutes   Cook Time: 3-4 Minutes   Serves: 1

Ingredients:

- 2 tablespoons strawberry cream cheese
- 1 tablespoon strawberry jam
- 1/2 cup fresh strawberries, sliced
- 1 tablespoon chopped pecans
- 2 teaspoons unsalted butter, at room temperature
- 2 slices strawberry swirl bread, cut into 4-inch circles

Directions:

1. Mix strawberry cream cheese and strawberry jam in a small bowl.
2. Preheat Breakfast Sandwich Maker until the green PREHEAT light comes on. Lift cover, top ring, and cooking plate.
3. Spread 1 teaspoon butter on one side of each strawberry swirl bread circle.
4. Flip bread circles over and spread 1 tablespoon of the cream cheese mixture on each slice.
5. Place one circle of strawberry swirl bread onto the bottom plate, buttered side down. Top with sliced fresh strawberries and chopped pecans.
6. Lower the top ring and cooking plate. Add the remaining strawberries and bread, buttered side up.
7. Close cover and cook for 3 to 4 minutes.
8. Slide out the cooking plate by rotating the handle clockwise. Lift cover and rings; carefully remove the sandwich with a plastic spatula.

Nutritional Value (Amount per Serving):

Calories: 219; Fat: 19.22; Carb: 10.24; Protein: 3.8

Apple Cinnamon Crunch Breakfast Sandwich

Prep Time: 10 Minutes   Cook Time: 3-4 Minutes   Serves: 1

Ingredients:

- 2 tablespoons cinnamon cream cheese
- 1 tablespoon apple butter
- 1/2 cup apple slices, thinly sliced

- 1 tablespoon granola
- 2 teaspoons unsalted butter, at room temperature
- 2 slices apple cinnamon bread, cut into 4-inch circles

Directions:

1. Combine cinnamon cream cheese and apple butter in a small bowl.
2. Preheat Breakfast Sandwich Maker until the green PREHEAT light comes on. Lift cover, top ring, and cooking plate.
3. Spread 1 teaspoon butter on one side of each apple cinnamon bread circle.
4. Flip bread circles over and spread 1 tablespoon of the cream cheese mixture on each slice.
5. Place one circle of apple cinnamon bread onto the bottom plate, buttered side down. Top with thinly sliced apple and granola.
6. Lower the top ring and cooking plate. Add the remaining apple slices and bread, buttered side up.
7. Close cover and cook for 3 to 4 minutes.
8. Slide out the cooking plate by rotating the handle clockwise. Lift cover and rings; carefully remove the sandwich with a plastic spatula.

Nutritional Value (Amount per Serving):

Calories: 1324; Fat: 68.95; Carb: 165.04; Protein: 18.7

Cherry Almond Delight Breakfast Sandwich

Prep Time: 15 Minutes   Cook Time: 3-4 Minutes   Serves: 1

Ingredients:

- 2 tablespoons almond-flavored cream cheese
- 1 tablespoon cherry preserves
- 1/2 cup fresh cherries, pitted and halved
- 1 tablespoon slivered almonds
- 2 teaspoons unsalted butter, at room temperature
- 2 slices almond cherry bread, cut into 4-inch circles

Directions:

1. Mix almond-flavored cream cheese and cherry preserves in a small bowl.
2. Preheat Breakfast Sandwich Maker until the green PREHEAT light comes on. Lift cover, top ring, and cooking plate.
3. Spread 1 teaspoon butter on one side of each almond cherry bread circle.
4. Flip bread circles over and spread 1 tablespoon of the cream cheese mixture on each slice.
5. Place one circle of almond cherry bread onto the bottom plate, buttered side down. Top with halved fresh cherries and slivered almonds.
6. Lower the top ring and cooking plate. Add the remaining cherries and

bread, buttered side up.

7. Close cover and cook for 3 to 4 minutes.
8. Slide out the cooking plate by rotating the handle clockwise. Lift cover and rings; carefully remove the sandwich with a plastic spatula.

Nutritional Value (Amount per Serving):

Calories: 201; Fat: 14.47; Carb: 16.15; Protein: 3.89

Plum Paradise Breakfast Sandwich

Prep Time: 12 Minutes   Cook Time: 3-4 Minutes   Serves: 1

Ingredients:

- 2 tablespoons vanilla almond butter
- 1 tablespoon plum jam
- 1/2 cup ripe plums, sliced
- 1 tablespoon sliced pistachios
- 2 teaspoons unsalted butter, at room temperature
- 2 slices almond plum bread, cut into 4-inch circles

Directions:

1. Combine vanilla almond butter and plum jam in a small bowl.
2. Preheat Breakfast Sandwich Maker until the green PREHEAT light comes on. Lift cover, top ring, and cooking plate.
3. Spread 1 teaspoon butter on one side of each almond plum bread circle.
4. Flip bread circles over and spread 1 tablespoon of the almond butter mixture on each slice.
5. Place one circle of almond plum bread onto the bottom plate, buttered side down. Top with sliced ripe plums and sliced pistachios.
6. Lower the top ring and cooking plate. Add the remaining plums and bread, buttered side up.
7. Close cover and cook for 3 to 4 minutes.
8. Slide out the cooking plate by rotating the handle clockwise. Lift cover and rings; carefully remove the sandwich with a plastic spatula.

Nutritional Value (Amount per Serving):

Calories: 524; Fat: 26.65; Carb: 70.19; Protein: 9.54

Mixed Melon Medley Breakfast Sandwich

Prep Time: 15 Minutes   Cook Time: 3-4 Minutes   Serves: 1

Ingredients:

- 2 tablespoons honeydew-flavored Greek yogurt

- 1 tablespoon watermelon jelly
- 1/2 cup mixed melon balls (honeydew, cantaloupe, watermelon)
- 1 tablespoon mint leaves, chopped
- 2 teaspoons unsalted butter, at room temperature
- 2 slices honeydew melon bread, cut into 4-inch circles

Directions:

1. Mix honeydew-flavored Greek yogurt and watermelon jelly in a small bowl.
2. Preheat Breakfast Sandwich Maker until the green PREHEAT light comes on. Lift cover, top ring, and cooking plate.
3. Spread 1 teaspoon butter on one side of each honeydew melon bread circle.
4. Flip bread circles over and spread 1 tablespoon of the yogurt mixture on each slice.
5. Place one circle of honeydew melon bread onto the bottom plate, buttered side down. Top with mixed melon balls and chopped mint leaves.
6. Lower the top ring and cooking plate. Add the remaining melon balls and bread, buttered side up.
7. Close cover and cook for 3 to 4 minutes.
8. Slide out the cooking plate by rotating the handle clockwise. Lift cover and rings; carefully remove the sandwich with a plastic spatula.

Nutritional Value (Amount per Serving):

Calories: 481; Fat: 8,56; Carb: 100.77; Protein: 11.88

Orange Creamsicle Breakfast Sandwich

Prep Time: 12 Minutes   Cook Time: 3-4 Minutes   Serves: 1

Ingredients:

- 2 tablespoons orange-flavored cream cheese
- 1 tablespoon orange marmalade
- 1/2 cup orange segments
- 1 tablespoon chopped macadamia nuts
- 2 teaspoons unsalted butter, at room temperature
- 2 slices orange zest swirl bread, cut into 4-inch circles

Directions:

1. Combine orange-flavored cream cheese and orange marmalade in a small bowl.
2. Preheat Breakfast Sandwich Maker until the green PREHEAT light comes on. Lift cover, top ring, and cooking plate.
3. Spread 1 teaspoon butter on one side of each orange zest swirl bread circle.
4. Flip bread circles over and spread 1 tablespoon of the cream cheese mixture on each slice.

5. Place one circle of orange zest swirl bread onto the bottom plate, buttered side down. Top with orange segments and chopped macadamia nuts.
6. Lower the top ring and cooking plate. Add the remaining orange segments and bread, buttered side up.
7. Close cover and cook for 3 to 4 minutes.
8. Slide out the cooking plate by rotating the handle clockwise. Lift cover and rings; carefully remove the sandwich with a plastic spatula.

Nutritional Value (Amount per Serving):

Calories: 366; Fat: 19.04; Carb: 46.02; Protein: 4.87

Blackberry Basil Bliss Breakfast Sandwich

Prep Time: 15 Minutes   Cook Time: 3-4 Minutes   Serves: 1

Ingredients:

- 2 tablespoons mascarpone cheese
- 1 tablespoon blackberry preserves
- 2 teaspoons unsalted butter, at room temperature
- 2 slices blackberry swirl bread, cut into 4-inch circles
- 1/2 cup fresh blackberries
- 1 tablespoon fresh basil, chopped

Directions:

1. Mix mascarpone cheese and blackberry preserves in a small bowl.
2. Preheat Breakfast Sandwich Maker until the green PREHEAT light comes on. Lift cover, top ring, and cooking plate.
3. Spread 1 teaspoon butter on one side of each blackberry swirl bread circle.
4. Flip bread circles over and spread 1 tablespoon of the mascarpone mixture on each slice.
5. Place one circle of blackberry swirl bread onto the bottom plate, buttered side down. Top with fresh blackberries and chopped basil.
6. Lower the top ring and cooking plate. Add the remaining blackberries and bread, buttered side up.
7. Close cover and cook for 3 to 4 minutes.
8. Slide out the cooking plate by rotating the handle clockwise. Lift cover and rings; carefully remove the sandwich with a plastic spatula.

Nutritional Value (Amount per Serving):

Calories: 398; Fat: 12.02; Carb: 68.75; Protein: 9.14

Grapefruit Ginger Zing Breakfast Sandwich

Prep Time: 12 Minutes   Cook Time: 3-4 Minutes   Serves: 1

Ingredients:

- 2 tablespoons ginger-infused cream cheese
- 1 tablespoon grapefruit marmalade
- 1/2 cup grapefruit segments
- 1 tablespoon candied ginger, finely chopped
- 2 teaspoons unsalted butter, at room temperature
- 2 slices grapefruit swirl bread, cut into 4-inch circles

Directions:

1. Combine ginger-infused cream cheese and grapefruit marmalade in a small bowl.
2. Preheat Breakfast Sandwich Maker until the green PREHEAT light comes on. Lift cover, top ring, and cooking plate.
3. Spread 1 teaspoon butter on one side of each grapefruit swirl bread circle.
4. Flip bread circles over and spread 1 tablespoon of the cream cheese mixture on each slice.
5. Place one circle of grapefruit swirl bread onto the bottom plate, buttered side down. Top with grapefruit segments and chopped candied ginger.
6. Lower the top ring and cooking plate. Add the remaining grapefruit segments and bread, buttered side up.
7. Close cover and cook for 3 to 4 minutes.
8. Slide out the cooking plate by rotating the handle clockwise. Lift cover and rings; carefully remove the sandwich with a plastic spatula.

Nutritional Value (Amount per Serving):

Calories: 346; Fat: 14.39; Carb: 54.16; Protein: 6.58

Mango Mint Madness Breakfast Sandwich

Prep Time: 15 Minutes   Cook Time: 3-4 Minutes   Serves: 1

Ingredients:

- 2 tablespoons mint-infused Greek yogurt
- 1 tablespoon mango chutney
- 1/2 cup diced fresh mango
- 1 tablespoon fresh mint leaves, chopped
- 2 teaspoons unsalted butter, at room temperature
- 2 slices mango mint swirl bread, cut into 4-inch circles

Directions:

1. Mix mint-infused Greek yogurt and mango chutney in a small bowl.
2. Preheat Breakfast Sandwich Maker until the green PREHEAT light comes on. Lift cover, top ring, and cooking plate.

3. Spread 1 teaspoon butter on one side of each mango mint swirl bread circle.
4. Flip bread circles over and spread 1 tablespoon of the yogurt mixture on each slice.
5. Place one circle of mango mint swirl bread onto the bottom plate, buttered side down. Top with diced fresh mango and chopped mint leaves.
6. Lower the top ring and cooking plate. Add the remaining mango and bread, buttered side up.
7. Close cover and cook for 3 to 4 minutes.
8. Slide out the cooking plate by rotating the handle clockwise. Lift cover and rings; carefully remove the sandwich with a plastic spatula.

Nutritional Value (Amount per Serving):

Calories: 216; Fat: 7.09; Carb: 38.56; Protein: 3.66

Cranberry Orange Crunch Breakfast Sandwich

Prep Time: 12 Minutes   Cook Time: 3-4 Minutes   Serves: 1

Ingredients:

- 2 tablespoons orange-infused cream cheese
- 1 tablespoon cranberry sauce
- 1/2 cup fresh cranberries
- 1 tablespoon granola
- 2 teaspoons unsalted butter, at room temperature
- 2 slices cranberry orange swirl bread, cut into 4-inch circles

Directions:

1. Combine orange-infused cream cheese and cranberry sauce in a small bowl.
2. Preheat Breakfast Sandwich Maker until the green PREHEAT light comes on. Lift cover, top ring, and cooking plate.
3. Spread 1 teaspoon butter on one side of each cranberry orange swirl bread circle.
4. Flip bread circles over and spread 1 tablespoon of the cream cheese mixture on each slice.
5. Place one circle of cranberry orange swirl bread onto the bottom plate, buttered side down. Top with fresh cranberries and granola.
6. Lower the top ring and cooking plate. Add the remaining cranberries and bread, buttered side up.
7. Close cover and cook for 3 to 4 minutes.
8. Slide out the cooking plate by rotating the handle clockwise. Lift cover and rings; carefully remove the sandwich with a plastic spatula.

Nutritional Value (Amount per Serving):

Calories: 520; Fat: 16.21; Carb: 94.24; Protein: 3.58

Chapter 8: Tea Sandwiches

Smoked Salmon and Cream Cheese Tea Sandwiches

Prep Time: 10 Minutes   Cook Time: 5 Minutes   Serves: 1

Ingredients:

- 2 tablespoons cream cheese
- Smoked salmon slices
- Capers
- Fresh dill
- 4 slices of pumpernickel bread

Directions:

1. Preheat the Breakfast Sandwich Maker until the green PREHEAT light comes on.
2. Spread cream cheese evenly on each slice of bread.
3. Layer smoked salmon on two of the bread slices.
4. Sprinkle capers and fresh dill over the salmon.
5. Place in the bottom ring of the Sandwich Maker.
6. Lower the cooking plate and the top ring.
7. Add the top slice of the sandwich onto the cooking plate.
8. Cook the sandwiches for 5 minutes.
9. Allow to cool slightly before serving.

Nutritional Value (Amount per Serving):

Calories: 372; Fat: 14.17; Carb: 45,72; Protein: 18.23

Egg Salad and Watercress Tea Sandwiches

Prep Time: 15 Minutes   Cook Time: 5 Minutes   Serves: 1

Ingredients:

- 2 hard-boiled eggs, chopped
- 2 tablespoons mayonnaise
- Chopped chives
- Watercress leaves
- Salt and pepper to taste
- 4 slices of white bread

Directions:

1. Preheat the Breakfast Sandwich Maker until the green PREHEAT light comes on.
2. In a bowl, mix chopped hard-boiled eggs, mayonnaise, chopped chives, salt, and pepper.
3. Spread the egg salad mixture evenly on each slice of bread.
4. Place watercress leaves on two of the bread slices.
5. Place in the bottom ring of the Sandwich Maker.
6. Lower the cooking plate and the top ring.
7. Add the top slice of the sandwich onto the cooking plate.
8. Cook the sandwiches for 5 minutes.

9. Allow to cool slightly before serving.

Nutritional Value (Amount per Serving):

   Calories: 1092; Fat: 24.04; Carb: 171.2; Protein: 43.12

Roasted Red Pepper and Hummus Tea Sandwiches

Prep Time: 12 Minutes   Cook Time: 6 Minutes   Serves: 1

Ingredients:

- 2 tablespoons hummus
- Roasted red pepper strips
- Kalamata olives, sliced
- Fresh basil leaves
- 4 slices of ciabatta bread

Directions:

1. Preheat the Breakfast Sandwich Maker until the green PREHEAT light comes on.
2. Spread hummus evenly on each slice of bread.
3. Layer roasted red pepper strips on two of the bread slices.
4. Sprinkle sliced Kalamata olives over the peppers.
5. Place fresh basil leaves on top.
6. Place in the bottom ring of the Sandwich Maker.
7. Lower the cooking plate and the top ring.
8. Add the top slice of the sandwich onto the cooking plate.
9. Cook the sandwiches for 6 minutes.
10. Allow to cool slightly before serving.

Nutritional Value (Amount per Serving):

   Calories: 290; Fat: 6.13; Carb: 49.11; Protein: 9

Turkey and Cranberry Tea Sandwiches

Prep Time: 10 Minutes   Cook Time: 5 Minutes   Serves: 1

Ingredients:

- 2 tablespoons cranberry sauce
- Thin turkey slices
- Cream cheese
- Baby spinach leaves
- 4 slices of whole wheat bread

Directions:

1. Preheat the Breakfast Sandwich Maker until the green PREHEAT light comes on.
2. Spread cranberry sauce evenly on each slice of bread.
3. Layer turkey slices on two of the bread slices.

4. Spread cream cheese on the other two slices.
5. Place baby spinach leaves over the cream cheese.
6. Place in the bottom ring of the Sandwich Maker.
7. Lower the cooking plate and the top ring.
8. Add the top slice of the sandwich onto the cooking plate.
9. Cook the sandwiches for 5 minutes.
10. Allow to cool slightly before serving.

Nutritional Value (Amount per Serving):

Calories: 767; Fat: 14.65; Carb: 141.6; Protein: 28.38

Avocado and Radish Tea Sandwiches

Prep Time: 10 Minutes   Cook Time: 5 Minutes   Serves: 1

Ingredients:

- 2 tablespoons mashed avocado
- Sliced radishes
- Microgreens
- Lemon zest
- Salt and pepper to taste
- 4 slices of whole grain bread

Directions:

1. Preheat the Breakfast Sandwich Maker until the green PREHEAT light comes on.
2. Spread mashed avocado evenly on each slice of bread.
3. Place sliced radishes on two of the bread slices.
4. Add a layer of microgreens over the radishes.
5. Sprinkle lemon zest, salt, and pepper.
6. Place in the bottom ring of the Sandwich Maker.
7. Lower the cooking plate and the top ring.
8. Add the top slice of the sandwich onto the cooking plate.
9. Cook the sandwiches for 5 minutes.
10. Allow to cool slightly before serving.

Nutritional Value (Amount per Serving):

Calories: 1107; Fat: 66.08; Carb: 112.97; Protein: 31.03

Roasted Tomato and Goat Cheese Tea Sandwiches

Prep Time: 15 Minutes   Cook Time: 5 Minutes   Serves: 1

Ingredients:

- 2 tablespoons goat cheese
- Roasted tomato slices
- Fresh basil leaves
- Balsamic glaze

- Salt and pepper to taste
- 4 slices of ciabatta bread

Directions:

1. Preheat the Breakfast Sandwich Maker until the green PREHEAT light comes on.
2. Spread goat cheese evenly on each slice of bread.
3. Place roasted tomato slices on two of the bread slices.
4. Add fresh basil leaves over the tomatoes.
5. Drizzle with balsamic glaze.
6. Season with salt and pepper.
7. Place in the bottom ring of the Sandwich Maker.
8. Lower the cooking plate and the top ring.
9. Add the top slice of the sandwich onto the cooking plate.
10. Cook the sandwiches for 5 minutes.
11. Allow to cool slightly before serving.

Nutritional Value (Amount per Serving):

Calories: 323; Fat: 8.19; Carb: 49.75; Protein: 13.66

Prosciutto and Fig Tea Sandwiches

Prep Time: 10 Minutes   Cook Time: 5 Minutes   Serves: 1

Ingredients:

- Fig jam
- Prosciutto slices
- Mascarpone cheese
- Baby arugula leaves
- 4 slices of baguette

Directions:

1. Preheat the Breakfast Sandwich Maker until the green PREHEAT light comes on.
2. Spread fig jam evenly on each slice of bread.
3. Layer prosciutto on two of the bread slices.
4. Spread mascarpone cheese on the other two slices.
5. Add baby arugula leaves over the cheese.
6. Place in the bottom ring of the Sandwich Maker.
7. Lower the cooking plate and the top ring.
8. Add the top slice of the sandwich onto the cooking plate.
9. Cook the sandwiches for 5 minutes.
10. Allow to cool slightly before serving.

Nutritional Value (Amount per Serving):

Calories: 1089; Fat: 46.22; Carb: 23.54; Protein: 149.66

Roasted Vegetable and Goat Cheese Tea Sandwiches

Prep Time: 15 Minutes   Cook Time: 6 Minutes   Serves: 1

Ingredients:

- 2 tablespoons goat cheese
- Roasted bell pepper strips
- Zucchini ribbons
- Fresh basil leaves
- 4 slices of multigrain bread

Directions:

1. Preheat the Breakfast Sandwich Maker until the green PREHEAT light comes on.
2. Spread goat cheese evenly on each slice of bread.
3. Layer roasted bell pepper strips on two of the bread slices.
4. Add zucchini ribbons over the peppers.
5. Place fresh basil leaves on top.
6. Place in the bottom ring of the Sandwich Maker.
7. Lower the cooking plate and the top ring.
8. Add the top slice of the sandwich onto the cooking plate.
9. Cook the sandwiches for 6 minutes.
10. Allow to cool slightly before serving.

Nutritional Value (Amount per Serving):

Calories: 297; Fat: 7.85; Carb: 44.46; Protein: 12.63

Pear and Blue Cheese Tea Sandwiches

Prep Time: 12 Minutes   Cook Time: 5 Minutes   Serves: 1

Ingredients:

- 2 tablespoons blue cheese
- Thin pear slices
- Honey
- Chopped walnuts
- 4 slices of walnut bread

Directions:

1. Preheat the Breakfast Sandwich Maker until the green PREHEAT light comes on.
2. Spread blue cheese evenly on each slice of bread.
3. Layer thin pear slices on two of the bread slices.
4. Drizzle honey over the pears.
5. Sprinkle chopped walnuts.
6. Place one bread in the bottom ring of the Sandwich Maker.
7. Lower the cooking plate and the top ring.
8. Add the top slice of the sandwich onto the cooking plate.

9. Cook the sandwich for 5 minutes.
10. Allow to cool slightly before serving.

Nutritional Value (Amount per Serving):

Calories: 1970; Fat: 191.34; Carb: 50.99; Protein: 46.84

Sundried Tomato and Mozzarella Tea Sandwiches

Prep Time: 10 Minutes   Cook Time: 5 Minutes   Serves: 1

Ingredients:

- 2 tablespoons sundried tomato pesto
- Fresh mozzarella slices
- Sundried tomatoes, chopped
- Fresh basil leaves
- 4 slices of ciabatta bread

Directions:

1. Preheat the Breakfast Sandwich Maker until the green PREHEAT light comes on.
2. Spread sundried tomato pesto evenly on each slice of bread.
3. Place fresh mozzarella slices on two of the bread slices.
4. Sprinkle chopped sundried tomatoes over the mozzarella.
5. Place fresh basil leaves on top.
6. Place one bread in the bottom ring of the Sandwich Maker.
7. Lower the cooking plate and the top ring.
8. Add the top slice of the sandwich onto the cooking plate.
9. Cook the sandwich for 5 minutes.
10. Allow to cool slightly before serving.

Nutritional Value (Amount per Serving):

Calories: 326; Fat: 6.67; Carb: 55.22; Protein: 12.31

Pesto Chicken Salad Tea Sandwiches

Prep Time: 15 Minutes   Cook Time: 6 Minutes   Serves: 1

Ingredients:

- 2 tablespoons pesto
- Chicken breast, cooked and shredded
- Cherry tomatoes, halved
- Fresh spinach leaves
- 4 slices of whole wheat bread

Directions:

1. Preheat the Breakfast Sandwich Maker until the green PREHEAT light comes on.
2. Spread pesto evenly on each slice of bread.

3. Mix shredded cooked chicken with halved cherry tomatoes.
4. Place the chicken mixture on two of the bread slices.
5. Add fresh spinach leaves over the mixture.
6. Place one bread in the bottom ring of the Sandwich Maker.
7. Lower the cooking plate and the top ring.
8. Add the top slice of the sandwich onto the cooking plate.
9. Cook the sandwich for 6 minutes.
10. Allow to cool slightly before serving.

Nutritional Value (Amount per Serving):

Calories: 919; Fat: 28.29; Carb: 97.14; Protein: 74.07

Turkey and Cranberry Chutney Tea Sandwiches

Prep Time: 12 Minutes   Cook Time: 6 Minutes   Serves: 1

Ingredients:

- 2 tablespoons cranberry chutney
- Thin turkey slices
- Brie cheese
- Pecans, chopped
- 4 slices of cranberry nut bread

Directions:

1. Preheat the Breakfast Sandwich Maker until the green PREHEAT light comes on.
2. Spread cranberry chutney evenly on each slice of bread.
3. Layer thin turkey slices on two of the bread slices.
4. Add slices of Brie cheese over the turkey.
5. Sprinkle chopped pecans.
6. Place one bread in the bottom ring of the Sandwich Maker.
7. Lower the cooking plate and the top ring.
8. Add the top slice of the sandwich onto the cooking plate.
9. Cook the sandwich for 6 minutes.
10. Allow to cool slightly before serving.

Nutritional Value (Amount per Serving):

Calories: 1224; Fat: 87.04; Carb: 108.55; Protein: 18.79

Roast Beef and Horseradish Tea Sandwiches

Prep Time: 10 Minutes   Cook Time: 5 Minutes   Serves: 1

Ingredients:

- 2 tablespoons horseradish sauce
- Thin slices of roast beef

- Swiss cheese slices
- Watercress leaves
- 4 slices of rye bread

Directions:

1. Preheat the Breakfast Sandwich Maker until the green PREHEAT light comes on.
2. Spread horseradish sauce evenly on each slice of bread.
3. Layer thin slices of roast beef on two of the bread slices.
4. Add Swiss cheese slices over the roast beef.
5. Place watercress leaves on top.
6. Place one bread in the bottom ring of the Sandwich Maker.
7. Lower the cooking plate and the top ring.
8. Add the top slice of the sandwich onto the cooking plate.
9. Cook the sandwich for 5 minutes.
10. Allow to cool slightly before serving.

Nutritional Value (Amount per Serving):

Calories: 849; Fat: 23.94; Carb: 131.71; Protein: 31.8

Caprese with Balsamic Glaze Tea Sandwiches

Prep Time: 10 Minutes   Cook Time: 5 Minutes   Serves: 1

Ingredients:

- 2 tablespoons balsamic glaze
- Fresh mozzarella slices
- Tomato slices
- Fresh basil leaves
- 4 slices of ciabatta bread

Directions:

1. Preheat the Breakfast Sandwich Maker until the green PREHEAT light comes on.
2. Drizzle balsamic glaze evenly on each slice of bread.
3. Place fresh mozzarella slices on two of the bread slices.
4. Add tomato slices over the mozzarella.
5. Place fresh basil leaves on top.
6. Place one bread in the bottom ring of the Sandwich Maker.
7. Lower the cooking plate and the top ring.
8. Add the top slice of the sandwich onto the cooking plate.
9. Cook the sandwich for 5 minutes.
10. Allow to cool slightly before serving.

Nutritional Value (Amount per Serving):

Calories: 331; Fat: 6.68; Carb: 56.4; Protein: 12.88

Chapter 9: Keto Sandwiches

Bacon, Egg, and Avocado Delight

Prep Time: 15 Minutes   Cook Time: 8 Minutes   Serves: 1

Ingredients:

- 2 slices Keto-friendly bread
- 2 slices cooked bacon
- 1 large egg, fried
- 1/2 avocado, sliced
- Salt and pepper to taste

Directions:

1. Preheat the Breakfast Sandwich Maker until the green PREHEAT light comes on.
2. Cook bacon and fry the egg simultaneously.
3. Place one slice of bread on the bottom ring.
4. Layer bacon, fried egg, and avocado on the bread.
5. Season with salt and pepper.
6. Lower cooking plate and the top ring.
7. Add the second slice of bread onto the cooking plate.
8. Cook for about 8 minutes or until the bread is toasted, and ingredients are warmed.

Nutritional Value (Amount per Serving):

Calories: 587; Fat: 43.4; Carb: 33.41; Protein: 19.23

Spinach and Salmon Delight

Prep Time: 15 Minutes   Cook Time: 8 Minutes   Serves: 1

Ingredients:

- 2 slices Keto-friendly bread
- 2 ounces smoked salmon
- 1/2 cup fresh spinach leaves
- 2 tablespoons cream cheese
- Lemon zest for garnish

Directions:

1. Preheat the Breakfast Sandwich Maker until the green PREHEAT light comes on.
2. Spread cream cheese on one side of each bread slice.
3. Place one slice of bread , cream cheese side down, on the bottom ring.
4. Layer smoked salmon and fresh spinach on the bread.
5. Top with the second slice of bread, cream cheese side up.
6. Lower cooking plate and the top ring.
7. Top with the second slice of bread, cream cheese side up.
8. Cook for about 8 minutes or until the bread is toasted, and the ingredients are warmed.

9. Garnish with lemon zest before serving.

Nutritional Value (Amount per Serving):

Calories: 296; Fat: 14.15; Carb: 24.67; Protein: 17.96

Zucchini and Mozzarella Wrap

Prep Time: 10 Minutes   Cook Time: 8 Minutes   Serves: 1

Ingredients:

- 2 large zucchini slices (for wrapping)
- 2 slices fresh mozzarella
- 1/4 cup cherry tomatoes, halved
- Fresh basil leaves
- Olive oil for drizzling

Directions:

1. Preheat the Breakfast Sandwich Maker until the green PREHEAT light comes on.
2. Lay the zucchini slices on the bottom ring, slightly overlapping.
3. Arrange mozzarella slices, cherry tomatoes, and basil on the zucchini.
4. Drizzle with olive oil.
5. Lower cooking plate and the top ring.
6. Add another layer of zucchini slices on top.
7. Cook for about 8 minutes or until the wrap is secured and ingredients are slightly warmed.

Nutritional Value (Amount per Serving):

Calories: 313; Fat: 16.02; Carb: 33.7; Protein: 14.28

Tuna Salad Collard Wrap

Prep Time: 15 Minutes   Cook Time: 8 Minutes   Serves: 1

Ingredients:

- 2 large collard green leaves (for wrapping)
- 1 can (5 ounces) tuna, drained
- 2 tablespoons mayonnaise (Keto-friendly)
- 1 tablespoon Dijon mustard
- 1/4 cup diced celery

Directions:

1. Preheat the Breakfast Sandwich Maker until the green PREHEAT light comes on.
2. Lay the collard green leaves on the bottom ring.
3. In a bowl, mix drained tuna, mayonnaise, Dijon mustard, and diced celery.

4. Divide the tuna salad mixture among the collard leaves.
5. Lower cooking plate and the top ring.
6. Add another layer of collard leaves on top.
7. Cook for about 8 minutes or until the collard leaves are slightly tender, and the filling is warmed.

Nutritional Value (Amount per Serving):

Calories: 261; Fat: 11.86; Carb: 4.12; Protein: 35.48

Egg and Avocado Collagen Wrap

Prep Time: 10 Minutes   Cook Time: 8 Minutes   Serves: 1

Ingredients:

- 2 collagen wraps (Keto-friendly)
- 2 hard-boiled eggs, sliced
- 1/2 avocado, sliced
- Salt and pepper to taste
- 1 tablespoon mayonnaise (Keto-friendly)

Directions:

1. Preheat the Breakfast Sandwich Maker until the green PREHEAT light comes on.
2. Lay one collagen wrap on the bottom ring.
3. Arrange sliced hard-boiled eggs and avocado on the wrap.
4. Season with salt and pepper.
5. Spread mayonnaise over the ingredients.
6. Lower cooking plate and the top ring.
7. Add the second collagen wrap on top.
8. Cook for about 8 minutes or until the wrap is crisp and ingredients are heated.

Nutritional Value (Amount per Serving):

Calories: 486; Fat: 34.85; Carb: 22.1; Protein: 24.15

Turkey and Cranberry Collagen Wrap

Prep Time: 12 Minutes   Cook Time: 10 Minutes   Serves: 1

Ingredients:

- 2 collagen wraps (Keto-friendly)
- 4 slices turkey breast
- 2 tablespoons cream cheese
- 2 tablespoons cranberry sauce (sugar-free)
- 1/4 cup chopped pecans

Directions:

1. Preheat the Breakfast Sandwich Maker until the green PREHEAT light comes on.
2. Lay one collagen wrap on the bottom ring.
3. Spread cream cheese on the wrap.
4. Arrange turkey slices and drizzle with cranberry sauce.
5. Sprinkle chopped pecans over the filling.
6. Lower cooking plate and the top ring.
7. Add the second collagen wrap on top.
8. Cook for about 10 minutes or until the wrap is crisp and ingredients are heated.

Nutritional Value (Amount per Serving):

Calories: 504; Fat: 32.52; Carb: 29.17; Protein: 26.58

Spinach and Bacon Egg Wrap

Prep Time: 15 Minutes   Cook Time: 8 Minutes   Serves: 1

Ingredients:

- 2 large collard green leaves (for wrapping)
- 2 slices cooked bacon
- 1 large egg, scrambled
- 1 cup fresh spinach leaves
- 1 tablespoon olive oil

Directions:

1. Preheat the Breakfast Sandwich Maker until the green PREHEAT light comes on.
2. Lay the collard green leaves on the bottom ring.
3. In a pan, sauté spinach with olive oil until wilted.
4. Place one slice of cooked bacon on each collard leaf.
5. Top with scrambled egg and sautéed spinach.
6. Lower cooking plate and the top ring.
7. Add another layer of collard leaves on top.
8. Cook for about 8 minutes or until the collard leaves are slightly tender, and the filling is warmed.

Nutritional Value (Amount per Serving):

Calories: 421; Fat: 37.39; Carb: 7.31; Protein: 15.66

Shrimp and Cucumber Collagen Wrap

Prep Time: 10 Minutes   Cook Time: 8 Minutes   Serves: 1

Ingredients:

- 2 collagen wraps (Keto-friendly)
- 6 cooked shrimp, peeled and deveined
- 1/2 cucumber, thinly sliced
- 2 tablespoons cream cheese
- Fresh dill for garnish

Directions:

1. Preheat the Breakfast Sandwich Maker until the green PREHEAT light comes on.
2. Lay one collagen wrap on the bottom ring.
3. Spread cream cheese on the wrap.
4. Arrange shrimp and cucumber slices on the wrap.
5. Garnish with fresh dill.
6. Lower cooking plate and the top ring.
7. Add the second collagen wrap on top.
8. Cook for about 8 minutes or until the wrap is crisp and ingredients are heated.

Nutritional Value (Amount per Serving):

Calories: 225; Fat: 13.81; Carb: 10.81; Protein: 14.82

Chicken Caesar Collard Wrap

Prep Time: 12 Minutes   Cook Time: 8 Minutes   Serves: 1

Ingredients:

- 2 large collard green leaves (for wrapping)
- 4 ounces grilled chicken, sliced
- 2 tablespoons Caesar dressing (Keto-friendly)
- 1/4 cup cherry tomatoes, halved
- 1/4 cup grated Parmesan cheese

Directions:

1. Preheat the Breakfast Sandwich Maker until the green PREHEAT light comes on.
2. Lay the collard green leaves on the bottom ring.
3. Arrange grilled chicken, cherry tomatoes, and Parmesan on the collard leaves.
4. Drizzle Caesar dressing over the ingredients.
5. Lower cooking plate and the top ring.
6. Add another layer of collard leaves on top.
7. Cook for about 8 minutes or until the wrap is secured, and ingredients are slightly warmed.

Nutritional Value (Amount per Serving):

Calories: 799; Fat: 70.45; Carb: 7.86; Protein: 32.57

Turkey Pesto Collagen Wrap

Prep Time: 12 Minutes   Cook Time: 8 Minutes   Serves: 1

Ingredients:

- 2 collagen wraps (Keto-friendly)
- 4 slices turkey breast
- 2 tablespoons pesto sauce (Keto-friendly)
- 1/4 cup sliced cherry tomatoes
- 2 tablespoons crumbled feta cheese

Directions:

1. Preheat the Breakfast Sandwich Maker until the green PREHEAT light comes on.
2. Lay one collagen wrap on the bottom ring.
3. Spread pesto sauce on the wrap.
4. Arrange turkey slices, cherry tomatoes, and crumbled feta on the wrap.
5. Lower cooking plate and the top ring.
6. Add the second collagen wrap on top.
7. Cook for about 8 minutes or until the wrap is crisp and ingredients are heated.

Nutritional Value (Amount per Serving):

Calories: 1156; Fat: 87.49; Carb: 25.11; Protein: 67.89

Tuna Avocado Collard Wrap

Prep Time: 15 Minutes   Cook Time: 8 Minutes   Serves: 1

Ingredients:

- 2 large collard green leaves (for wrapping)
- 1 can (5 ounces) tuna, drained
- 1/2 avocado, mashed
- 1 tablespoon mayonnaise (Keto-friendly)
- Salt and pepper to taste

Directions:

1. Preheat the Breakfast Sandwich Maker until the green PREHEAT light comes on.
2. Lay the collard green leaves on the bottom ring.
3. In a bowl, mix drained tuna, mashed avocado, mayonnaise, salt, and pepper.
4. Divide the tuna mixture among the collard leaves.
5. Lower cooking plate and the top ring.
6. Add another layer of collard leaves on top.

7. Cook for about 8 minutes or until the collard leaves are slightly tender, and the filling is warmed.

Nutritional Value (Amount per Serving):

Calories: 387; Fat: 21.52; Carb: 16.36; Protein: 37.59

Smoked Salmon and Cream Cheese Collagen Wrap

Prep Time: 10 Minutes   Cook Time: 8 Minutes   Serves: 1

Ingredients:

- 2 collagen wraps (Keto-friendly)
- 2 ounces smoked salmon
- 2 tablespoons cream cheese
- 1 tablespoon capers
- Fresh dill for garnish

Directions:

1. Preheat the Breakfast Sandwich Maker until the green PREHEAT light comes on.
2. Lay one collagen wrap on the bottom ring.
3. Spread cream cheese on the wrap.
4. Arrange smoked salmon and capers on the wrap.
5. Garnish with fresh dill.
6. Lower cooking plate and the top ring.
7. Add the second collagen wrap on top.
8. Cook for about 8 minutes or until the wrap is crisp and ingredients are heated.

Nutritional Value (Amount per Serving):

Calories: 294; Fat: 17.69; Carb: 11.15; Protein: 22.78

Chapter 10: Cheese Sandwiches

Caprese Panini

Prep Time: 12 Minutes   Cook Time: 5 Minutes   Serves: 1

Ingredients:

- 2 slices Italian bread
- 1 slice mozzarella cheese
- Tomato slices
- Fresh basil leaves
- Balsamic glaze
- 1 large egg, lightly scrambled
- Olive oil for brushing
- Salt and pepper to taste

Directions:

1. Preheat the Breakfast Sandwich Maker until the green PREHEAT light comes on.
2. Lift the cover, top ring, and cooking plate.
3. Brush olive oil on one side of each slice of Italian bread.
4. Place one slice of bread, oil side down, in the bottom ring.
5. Add mozzarella cheese, tomato slices, and fresh basil leaves. Drizzle with balsamic glaze.
6. Lower the cooking plate and top ring. Pour the scrambled egg over the ingredients. Season with salt and pepper.
7. Top with the remaining slice of bread, oil side up.
8. Close the cover and cook for 5 minutes.
9. Slide out the cooking plate by rotating the handle clockwise. Lift the cover and rings; carefully remove the sandwich.

Nutritional Value (Amount per Serving):

Calories: 285; Fat: 13.8; Carb: 31.1; Protein: 10.72

BBQ Pulled Pork Panini

Prep Time: 15 Minutes   Cook Time: 5 Minutes   Serves: 1

Ingredients:

- 1 ciabatta roll, halved
- 1 slice cheddar cheese
- BBQ pulled pork
- Coleslaw
- 1 large egg, lightly beaten
- Pickles
- Salt and pepper to taste

Directions:

1. Preheat the Breakfast Sandwich Maker until the green PREHEAT light comes on.
2. Lift the cover, top ring, and cooking plate.
3. Place the bottom half of the ciabatta roll, cut-side up.
4. Add cheddar cheese, a portion of BBQ pulled pork, and coleslaw.

5. Lower the cooking plate and top ring. Pour the beaten egg over the ingredients. Season with salt and pepper.
6. Top with pickles.
7. Close the cover and cook for 5 minutes.
8. Slide out the cooking plate by rotating the handle clockwise. Lift the cover and rings; carefully remove the sandwich.

Nutritional Value (Amount per Serving):

Calories: 459; Fat: 23.55; Carb: 32; Protein: 29.86

Apple and Brie Panini

Prep Time: 10 Minutes   Cook Time: 5 Minutes   Serves: 1

Ingredients:

- 2 slices sourdough bread
- 1 slice Brie cheese
- Thinly sliced apple
- Honey
- 1 large egg, lightly scrambled
- Fresh thyme leaves
- Salt and pepper to taste

Directions:

1. Preheat the Breakfast Sandwich Maker until the green PREHEAT light comes on.
2. Lift the cover, top ring, and cooking plate.
3. Place one slice of sourdough bread in the bottom ring.
4. Add Brie cheese, thinly sliced apple, and a drizzle of honey.
5. Lower the cooking plate and top ring. Pour the scrambled egg over the ingredients. Season with salt, pepper, and fresh thyme leaves.
6. Top with the remaining slice of sourdough bread.
7. Close the cover and cook for 5 minutes.
8. Slide out the cooking plate by rotating the handle clockwise. Lift the cover and rings; carefully remove the sandwich.

Nutritional Value (Amount per Serving):

Calories: 408; Fat: 13.7; Carb: 62.06; Protein: 14

BLT Avocado Wrap

Prep Time: 10 Minutes   Cook Time: 5 Minutes   Serves: 1

Ingredients:

- 1 spinach wrap
- 1 slice provolone cheese
- 3 slices bacon, cooked
- Lettuce leaves

- Tomato slices
- Avocado, sliced
- 1 large egg, lightly beaten
- Ranch dressing
- Salt and pepper to taste

Directions:

1. Preheat the Breakfast Sandwich Maker until the green PREHEAT light comes on.
2. Lift the cover, top ring, and cooking plate.
3. Place the spinach wrap on the bottom ring.
4. Add provolone cheese, cooked bacon, lettuce, tomato slices, and sliced avocado.
5. Lower the cooking plate and top ring. Pour the beaten egg over the ingredients. Season with salt and pepper.
6. Drizzle with ranch dressing.
7. Close the cover and cook for 5 minutes.
8. Slide out the cooking plate by rotating the handle clockwise. Lift the cover and rings; carefully remove the wrap.

Nutritional Value (Amount per Serving):

Calories: 862; Fat: 74.65; Carb: 30.93; Protein: 26.6

Tuna Melt Panini

Prep Time: 10 Minutes   Cook Time: 5 Minutes   Serves: 1

Ingredients:

- 2 slices rye bread
- 1 slice Swiss cheese
- Tuna salad
- Red onion slices
- 1 large egg, lightly scrambled
- Pickles
- Salt and pepper to taste

Directions:

1. Preheat the Breakfast Sandwich Maker until the green PREHEAT light comes on.
2. Lift the cover, top ring, and cooking plate.
3. Place one slice of rye bread in the bottom ring.
4. Add Swiss cheese, a portion of tuna salad, and red onion slices.
5. Lower the cooking plate and top ring. Pour the scrambled egg over the ingredients. Season with salt and pepper.
6. Top with pickles.
7. Close the cover and cook for 5 minutes.
8. Slide out the cooking plate by rotating the handle clockwise. Lift the cover and rings; carefully remove the sandwich.

Nutritional Value (Amount per Serving):

Calories: 618; Fat: 17.4; Carb: 97.49; Protein: 22.33

Spinach and Artichoke Grilled Cheese

Prep Time: 10 Minutes   Cook Time: 5 Minutes   Serves: 1

Ingredients:

- 2 slices sourdough bread
- 1 slice mozzarella cheese
- Spinach and artichoke dip
- 1 large egg, lightly scrambled
- Sun-dried tomatoes, sliced
- Salt and pepper to taste

Directions:

1. Preheat the Breakfast Sandwich Maker until the green PREHEAT light comes on.
2. Lift the cover, top ring, and cooking plate.
3. Place one slice of sourdough bread in the bottom ring.
4. Add mozzarella cheese and a generous portion of spinach and artichoke dip.
5. Lower the cooking plate and top ring. Pour the scrambled egg over the ingredients. Season with salt and pepper.
6. Top with sun-dried tomatoes.
7. Close the cover and cook for 5 minutes.
8. Slide out the cooking plate by rotating the handle clockwise. Lift the cover and rings; carefully remove the sandwich.

Nutritional Value (Amount per Serving):

Calories: 282; Fat: 12.26; Carb: 32.92; Protein: 12.3

Turkey Pesto Panini

Prep Time: 10 Minutes   Cook Time: 5 Minutes   Serves: 1

Ingredients:

- 1 ciabatta roll, halved
- 1 slice provolone cheese
- 3 slices turkey breast
- Pesto sauce
- Tomato slices
- 1 large egg, lightly scrambled
- Fresh basil leaves
- Salt and pepper to taste

Directions:

1. Preheat the Breakfast Sandwich Maker until the green PREHEAT light comes on.
2. Lift the cover, top ring, and cooking plate.

3. Place the bottom half of the ciabatta roll, cut-side up.
4. Add provolone cheese, turkey slices, a spread of pesto sauce, and tomato slices.
5. Lower the cooking plate and top ring. Pour the beaten egg over the ingredients. Season with salt and pepper.
6. Top with fresh basil leaves.
7. Close the cover and cook for 5 minutes.
8. Slide out the cooking plate by rotating the handle clockwise. Lift the cover and rings; carefully remove the panini.

Nutritional Value (Amount per Serving):

Calories: 358; Fat: 14.49; Carb: 32.51; Protein: 24.31

Veggie Ranch Wrap

Prep Time: 12 Minutes   Cook Time: 5 Minutes   Serves: 1

Ingredients:

- 1 whole wheat wrap
- 1 slice cheddar cheese
- Hummus
- Sliced bell peppers (assorted colors)
- Sliced cucumber
- 1 large egg, lightly beaten
- Ranch dressing
- Salt and pepper to taste

Directions:

1. Preheat the Breakfast Sandwich Maker until the green PREHEAT light comes on.
2. Lift the cover, top ring, and cooking plate.
3. Place the whole wheat wrap on the bottom ring.
4. Add cheddar cheese, a spread of hummus, and sliced bell peppers and cucumber.
5. Lower the cooking plate and top ring. Pour the beaten egg over the ingredients. Season with salt and pepper.
6. Drizzle with ranch dressing.
7. Close the cover and cook for 5 minutes.
8. Slide out the cooking plate by rotating the handle clockwise. Lift the cover and rings; carefully remove the wrap.

Nutritional Value (Amount per Serving):

Calories: 598; Fat: 24.16; Carb: 76.59; Protein: 24.98

Hawaiian BBQ Chicken Panini

Prep Time: 10 Minutes   Cook Time: 5 Minutes   Serves: 1

Ingredients:

- 1 Hawaiian sweet roll, halved
- 1 slice pepper jack cheese
- Shredded BBQ chicken
- Pineapple ring, grilled
- 1 large egg, lightly scrambled
- BBQ sauce
- Salt and pepper to taste

Directions:

1. Preheat the Breakfast Sandwich Maker until the green PREHEAT light comes on.
2. Lift the cover, top ring, and cooking plate.
3. Place the bottom half of the Hawaiian sweet roll, cut-side up.
4. Add pepper jack cheese, shredded BBQ chicken, and a grilled pineapple ring.
5. Lower the cooking plate and top ring. Pour the beaten egg over the cooking plate. Season with salt and pepper.
6. Drizzle with BBQ sauce and add top half of the roll.
7. Close the cover and cook for 5 minutes.
8. Slide out the cooking plate by rotating the handle clockwise. Lift the cover and rings; carefully remove the panini.

Nutritional Value (Amount per Serving):

Calories: 530; Fat: 27.32; Carb: 43.6; Protein: 29.45

Caprese Flatbread

Prep Time: 12 Minutes   Cook Time: 5 Minutes   Serves: 1

Ingredients:

- 1 flatbread, halved
- 1 slice mozzarella cheese
- Tomato slices
- Fresh basil leaves
- Balsamic glaze
- 1 large egg, lightly beaten
- Olive oil for brushing
- Salt and pepper to taste

Directions:

1. Preheat the Breakfast Sandwich Maker until the green PREHEAT light comes on.
2. Lift the cover, top ring, and cooking plate.
3. Brush olive oil on one side of each half of the flatbread.
4. Place one half of the flatbread, oil side down, in the bottom ring.
5. Add mozzarella cheese, tomato slices, and fresh basil leaves. Drizzle with balsamic glaze.
6. Lower the cooking plate and top ring. Pour the beaten egg over the cooking plate. Season with salt and pepper.

7. Top with the remaining half of the flatbread, oil side up.
8. Close the cover and cook for 5 minutes.
9. Slide out the cooking plate by rotating the handle clockwise. Lift the cover and rings; carefully remove the flatbread.

Nutritional Value (Amount per Serving):

Calories: 515; Fat: 23.14; Carb: 59.85; Protein: 19.14

Southwest Chicken Wrap

Prep Time: 10 Minutes   Cook Time: 5 Minutes   Serves: 1

Ingredients:

- 1 spinach wrap
- 1 slice cheddar cheese
- Grilled chicken strips
- Black bean and corn salsa
- Avocado, sliced
- 1 large egg, lightly beaten
- Sour cream for drizzling
- Salt and pepper to taste

Directions:

1. Preheat the Breakfast Sandwich Maker until the green PREHEAT light comes on.
2. Lift the cover, top ring, and cooking plate.
3. Place the spinach wrap on the bottom ring.
4. Add cheddar cheese, grilled chicken strips, black bean and corn salsa, and sliced avocado.
5. Lower the cooking plate and top ring. Pour the beaten egg over the cooking plate. Season with salt and pepper.
6. Drizzle with sour cream.
7. Close the cover and cook for 5 minutes.
8. Slide out the cooking plate by rotating the handle clockwise. Lift the cover and rings; carefully remove the wrap.

Nutritional Value (Amount per Serving):

Calories: 1090; Fat: 91.37; Carb: 31.91; Protein: 44.49

Philly Cheesesteak Wrap

Prep Time: 12 Minutes   Cook Time: 5 Minutes   Serves: 1

Ingredients:

- 1 whole wheat wrap
- 1 slice provolone cheese
- Thinly sliced steak, cooked
- Sautéed bell peppers and onions
- 1 large egg, lightly scrambled
- Salt and pepper to taste

Directions:

1. Preheat the Breakfast Sandwich Maker until the green PREHEAT light comes on.
2. Lift the cover, top ring, and cooking plate.
3. Place the whole wheat wrap on the bottom ring.
4. Add provolone cheese, thinly sliced steak, and sautéed bell peppers and onions.
5. Lower the cooking plate and top ring. Pour the scrambled egg over the cooking plate. Season with salt and pepper.
6. Close the cover and cook for 5 minutes.
7. Slide out the cooking plate by rotating the handle clockwise. Lift the cover and rings; carefully remove the wrap.

Nutritional Value (Amount per Serving):

Calories: 741; Fat: 26.72; Carb: 72.29; Protein: 59.46

Bacon, Egg, and Gouda Croissant

Prep Time: 10 Minutes   Cook Time: 5 Minutes   Serves: 1

Ingredients:

- 1 croissant, halved
- 1 slice Gouda cheese
- 2 slices bacon, cooked
- 1 large egg, lightly scrambled
- Fresh arugula
- Salt and pepper to taste

Directions:

1. Preheat the Breakfast Sandwich Maker until the green PREHEAT light comes on.
2. Lift the cover, top ring, and cooking plate.
3. Place the bottom half of the croissant, cut-side up.
4. Add Gouda cheese, cooked bacon, and fresh arugula.
5. Lower the cooking plate and top ring. Pour the scrambled egg over the cooking plate. Season with salt and pepper.
6. Top with the remaining half of the croissant, cut-side down.
7. Close the cover and cook for 5 minutes.
8. Slide out the cooking plate by rotating the handle clockwise. Lift the cover and rings; carefully remove the croissant.

Nutritional Value (Amount per Serving):

Calories: 564; Fat: 41.21; Carb: 29.04; Protein: 20.29

APPENDIX RECIPE INDEX

Made in United States
Troutdale, OR
12/12/2024

26349246R20062